Poetry Says It Better

Poetry Says It Better

Poems to Help You Wake Up

Ellen Burstyn

HARPERONE

An Imprint of HarperCollins*Publishers*

The credits on page 247 constitute a continuation of this copyright page.

HarperCollins books may be purchased for educational, business, or sales promotional use. For information, please email the Special Markets Department at SPsales@harpercollins.com.

hc.com

FIRST EDITION

Designed by Bonni Leon-Berman
Photographs courtesy of the author.
Title page art by AIM HIGH 5, 2021 © Julia di Sano.
All rights reserved 2025/Bridgeman Images Whirling Dervishes

Library of Congress Cataloging-in-Publication Data has been applied for.

ISBN 978-0-06-338768-3

Printed in the United States of America

26 27 28 29 30 LBC 5 4 3 2 1

Dear Reader,

This is not a political book. It's about poetry and therefore about art. But I do think one of our politicians said this better than I could ever say it. This is from a speech President John F. Kennedy gave at Amherst College on October 26, 1963:

> When power leads men towards arrogance, poetry reminds him of his limitations. When power narrows the areas of man's concern, poetry reminds him of the richness and diversity of his existence. When power corrupts, poetry cleanses. For art establishes the basic human truth which must serve as the touchstone of our judgment.
>
> The artist, however faithful to his personal vision of reality, becomes the last champion of the individual mind and sensibility against an intrusive society and an officious state. The great artist is thus a solitary figure. He has, as Frost said, a lover's quarrel with the world. In pursuing his perceptions of reality, he must often sail against the currents of his time. This is not a popular role. . . .
>
> If sometimes our great artists have been the most critical of our society, it is because their sensitivity and their concern for justice, which must motivate any true artist, makes him aware that our Nation falls short of its highest potential. I see little of more importance to the future of our country and our civilization than full recognition of the place of the artist.

If art is to nourish the roots of our culture, society must set the artist free to follow his vision wherever it takes him. We must never forget that art is not a form of propaganda; it is a form of truth. And as Mr. MacLeish once remarked of poets, there is nothing worse for our trade than to be in style. In free society art is not a weapon and it does not belong to the spheres of polemic and ideology. Artists are not engineers of the soul. It may be different elsewhere. But democratic society—in it, the highest duty of the writer, the composer, the artist is to remain true to himself and to let the chips fall where they may. In serving his vision of the truth, the artist best serves his nation. And the nation which disdains the mission of art invites the fate of Robert Frost's hired man, the fate of having "nothing to look backward to with pride, and nothing to look forward to with hope."

Ellen Burstyn

My love of poetry as well as my love of travel have taken me many places. Here I am enjoying the monk's view from a mountain.

Poetry Says It Better

On the previous page,

Poetry seems to me to be an altered state. One of my Sufi teachers taught me how to do "the turn," another altered state. The dervishes stand on their left foot, with their big toe and next toe on either side of a nail in the ground and with their right foot crossing over their left foot they turn. Keeping their toes on either side of the nail keeps them in one place. The right arm is raised to the heavens or the upper atmosphere and channels the energy down through the dancers and the left arm sends it into the ground, so the energy travels through them in one arm and out the other as they are doing the turning. They get into an altered state as they're turning.

I AM AN ACTRESS, NOT A POET, but I am a lover of poetry. I have been since high school when I read a poem for the first time . . . well, not quite the first poem. *The Tales of Mother Goose* could be considered poetry, in a way, I guess. You see, in my home there were not only no poems, there were no books. One Christmas my aunt and uncle gave me a copy of *Heidi* as a present. I treasured that book for years.

I was sent to boarding school at age six. I turned seven there and was asked to take part in the Christmas program by reciting:

Little Miss Muffet,
Sat on a tuffet,
Eating her curds and whey;
Along came a spider,
Who sat down beside her,
And frightened Miss Muffet away.

I did not know what a tuffet was, had never heard of those curds and whey, but 'twas the first time I'd heard anything rhyme and learned that words knew how to play.

That's what it seems like to me. That the words are in a playful relationship to one another, when they rhyme or create a rhythm, or conjure a picture in my mind that refers to something that wasn't stated in the poem but underlies the words.

Oh, that's a good word! Isn't it? *Underlies.* Yes, that's what poetry does. It refers to what's not overtly being said but is better understood by referring to it in a creative way, that transmits a feeling that is looking for a home in the heart of a reader. Poetry, especially great poetry, pierces the heart of the reader via their imagination. Sometimes the words are meant to be at face value but not always in poetry. It is about the imagination.

᠅

I love poetry, as I've written. I'm writing this book for people who don't. Why?

Because I think they are missing out on something really good . . . good for their hearts—what Mary Oliver called "that organ of the emotions." I find that poems nourish something that helps our spirits soar.

I think people are often afraid of poetry. They might think they won't understand it. That it's too difficult, or too corny. What I've always found in poetry is wisdom. As you read on, you'll see I am trying to remember how I felt when I first read each of these poems and how they influenced me, and I hope you will also relate to them in a way that is more meaningful for you. You can turn to any page in the book and see what you get!

I want to begin with the very first poem that hooked me. In high school we were assigned to learn "Invictus" by William Ernest Henley, and that poem spoke to my core.

Invictus
William Ernest Henley

Out of the night that covers me,
   Black as the pit from pole to pole,
I thank whatever gods may be
   For my unconquerable soul.

In the fell clutch of circumstance
   I have not winced nor cried aloud.
Under the bludgeonings of chance
   My head is bloody, but unbowed.

Beyond this place of wrath and tears
   Looms but the Horror of the shade,
And yet the menace of the years
   Finds and shall find me unafraid.

It matters not how strait the gate,
   How charged with punishments the scroll,
I am the master of my fate,
   I am the captain of my soul.

Those last two lines went deep into my psyche as a teenager and empowered me with a way to relate to my own difficult circumstances, which included problems with my stepfather, who hated my mother's two children, which you'll read about later in the book. Poetry's wisdom, through metaphor, rhythm, and rhyme, can permeate the reader's core being.

Henley was twenty-six when he wrote "Invictus" and suffering from tuberculosis. I was sixteen, living in Detroit in a house where I didn't feel wanted, when I first read the poem. Those differences mattered not at all. And how did his words make me feel?

"I am the master of my fate!" Oh I see! "I am the captain of my soul!" Yes! Yes! I am free!

That began my real education, that poem. I didn't go to university; as a matter of fact, I didn't graduate high school. But I have been profoundly guided by many teachers of different kinds, and I have to say, one of the most profound teachers is poetry. I should probably (immodestly) add that despite my lack of formal education I have managed to be awarded four master's degrees.

I recently read that Clint Eastwood made a film called *Invictus*. So, I watched it and discovered it was about Nelson Mandela and "Invictus" was his favorite poem.

Mandela was arrested and imprisoned in 1962 for his anti-apartheid activism. He served more than twenty-seven years in prison. He has said that during those years when he felt his courage dim and depression descend, he would recite that poem to himself. After he was released from prison, he became the first Black elected president of South Africa.

He certainly did become the master of his fate and the captain of not only his own soul but also the soul of his whole beloved country, South Africa. I wish I'd had the chance to meet him. He sounds like a real poetry lover too.

♪

When I listen to great music, it feels like my ears have become passageways to my heart.

And when I read poetry, it seems that poetry is the music of language and language is the tool of consciousness.

I have memorized poems all my adult life. I carry an inner library around with me, and many times, something I see on my morning walk or something I hear during the day will sprout a poem, or part of a poem, inside me and send me, enriched, as I go on my way.

But not everyone is familiar with poetry.

I work with a beautiful, smart trainer named Wendy. One day, I had an impulse to share a poem with her. I asked, "Do you read poetry?" She answered, "No," in a slightly derisive tone.

When we left the gym and went up to my apartment before saying goodbye, I read to her a Mary Oliver poem. At the end, Wendy said, "Well, that's not sappy."

I thought, *Oh, dear! She thinks poetry is "Roses are red, violets are blue"!*

I thought about the pleasure I get from reading poetry and wondered how many people aren't aware of how much wisdom and just plain fun there is in poetry.

That became the seed for writing this book.

One of the things I love about poetry is the way poets see. Their gaze penetrates the surface and goes to the heart of things. It's not just the object being looked at—it's more what the poetic gaze illuminates about the meaning of the object, whether it's a flower, a path, a door, or a feeling.

The Poet
David Whyte

moves forward
to that edge
but lives sensibly,

through the senses
not because of them.

Above all he watches
where he steps.
As if it matters
where he leaves his prints.

The senses overwhelm him
at his peril.

Though he *must* be taken
by something greater.
That is what he uses
senses to perceive.

The poet's

task is simple.
He looks for quiet,
and speaks to what
he finds there.

But like Blake
in his engraving shop, works
with the fierceness
of acid on metal.

Melting apparent
surfaces away
and displaying
the infinite
which was hid.

In the early morning
he listens
by the window,
makes
the first utterance
and tries to overhear
himself
say something,
from which
in that silence,
it is impossible to retreat.

I want to share the consciousness-raising wisdom and pure pleasure of reading poetry with my fellow poetry lovers—but even more I hope I can introduce poetry to those who haven't yet discovered how poetry can enrich both their minds and their hearts.

I was still in high school when I was introduced to the poetry of Edna St. Vincent Millay. The way that came about was, I wrote a poem. I didn't know if it was any good or not, so I gave it to the smartest boy in class and asked him to tell me what he thought of it.

He read it and answered, "Just because your name is Edna doesn't mean you should copy her style." (My original name was Edna Rae Gillooly.)

"Whose style?" I asked.

"Edna St. Vincent Millay," he said.

When I read her poetry, she instantly became my favorite poet and remained so for many years. However, I have to say there was no copying her style; I wasn't capable of that. I offer my poem here, which I wrote at age fifteen, simply to give an idea of what my life was like as I was discovering poetry:

It's always darkest before the sunrise.
But my brightest hellos
are followed by the darkest goodbyes.
Each day when I wake, I say
today the darkness will break.
But each day I do believe

I am tempted to secede
from the throngs of hopeful souls
slowly approaching their goals.
Everything is so stark.
The cloak of happiness comes not in my size.
Everything is so dark.
And still the damn sun won't rise.

A howl of pain does not a good poem make. Here's Millay dealing
with the same emotional state. . . .

Departure
Edna St. Vincent Millay

It's little I care what path I take,
And where it leads it's little I care;
But out of this house, lest my heart break,
I must go, and off somewhere.

It's little I know what's in my heart,
What's in my mind it's little I know,
But there's that in me must up and start,
And it's little I care where my feet go.

I wish I could walk for a day and a night,
And find me at dawn in a desolate place
With never the rut of a road in sight,
Or the roof of a house, or the eyes of a face.

I wish I could walk till my blood should spout,
And drop me, never to stir again,
On a shore that is wide, for the tide is out,
And the weedy rocks are bare to the rain.

But dump or dock, where the path I take
Brings up, it's little enough I care,
And it's little I'd mind the fuss they'll make,
Huddled dead in a ditch somewhere.

"Is something the matter, dear," she said,
"That you sit at your work so silently?"
"No, mother, no—'twas a knot in my thread.
There goes the kettle—I'll make the tea."

I didn't read this particular Millay poem while still in high school. It was later, but I just loved it right away. I could identify with the rage that was being repressed and not ever allowed to be expressed. And then in the last verse, there is a change of font that expresses the outer reality as opposed to the unexpressed fury of the rest of the poem. I have never seen writing that better expresses suppressed rage like this one does.

Millay often assumed a character and then wrote in that character's voice, kind of like what an actress does. Here is another poem of hers, "Daphne."

Daphne
Edna St. Vincent Millay

Why do you follow me?—
Any moment I can be
Nothing but a laurel-tree.

Any moment of the chase
I can leave you in my place
A pink bough for your embrace.

Yet if over hill and hollow
Still it is your will to follow,
I am off;—to heel, Apollo!

She assumed the voice of the nymph Daphne, who in Greek mythology was being pursued by the god Apollo. Too bad some of the modern nymphs being pursued by insistent bosses don't have the ability to turn themselves into laurel trees—symbolically, that is.

In the myth when Daphne turns herself into a laurel tree and therefore avoids giving in to the god's desire, it is such a triumph that the laurel leaves woven into a crown became the symbol of victory for conquering heroes and heroines as well as winning Olympic athletes.

When I first encountered this poem, I didn't know that one day I would stand in front of the magnificent statue by Bernini that depicts in white marble the moment Apollo touches Daphne and she begins sprouting the roots, limbs, and leaves of the laurel tree. It's in the Villa Borghese in Rome, and I remember that its beauty and magnificent artistry brought tears to my eyes when I first saw it in 1970, when I lived in Rome for the better part of the year.

As I stood gazing at this magnificent realization in art of the myth of Daphne and Apollo, this poem that I had memorized decades earlier unfurled itself in my mind. What do I mean by "unfurled itself"? It's like I hear the first line, "Why do you follow me?" perhaps in my own voice, as though I am remembering.

Then almost like a scroll opening and revealing the next phrase, "Any moment I can be / Nothing but a laurel-tree." That line begins to reveal a bit of attitude on the part of Daphne. Then coming faster now, "Any moment of the chase / I can leave you in my place." Now I see her beginning to turn: "A pink bough for your embrace." Then still looking at Bernini's statue, I hear her voice low, "Yet if over hill and hollow / Still it is your wish to follow," she is turning away now, "I am off," then throwing over her shoulder in a saucy voice, "to heel, Apollo!"

✒

I just remembered another poem by Millay on the subject of love that I want to share with you.

Not in a silver casket cool with pearls
Edna St. Vincent Millay

Not in a silver casket cool with pearls
Or rich with red corundum or with blue,
Locked, and the key withheld, as other girls
Have given their loves, I give my love to you;
Not in a lovers'-knot, not in a ring
Worked in such fashion, and the legend plain—
Semper fidelis, where a secret spring
Kennels a drop of mischief for the brain:
Love in the open hand, no thing but that,
Ungemmed, unhidden, wishing not to hurt,
As one should bring you cowslips in a hat
Swung from the hand, or apples in her skirt,
I bring you, calling out as children do:
"Look what I have!—And these are all for you."

When I read this, I thought that her view of love was what I hoped I would be able to embrace. No clinging, no demanding, just giving or sharing, like apples from my skirt. But that turns out to be a very advanced stage of spiritual development. It is not that simple, is it?

I was in love with all three of my husbands. I remember the feeling so well, so fondly. I remember walking down the street realizing I was "in love." The feeling was like a blessing; I felt like I was caressed by a warm divine light. None of those beloveds still walk the planet.

I live without love now. I don't actively mind it. I'm past that. But recently I was attending an opening and saw an actor I've worked with in the past. We greeted each other in a friendly manner, then I asked, "How are you?" in a tone that was really asking, not a tone that gets a "fine, thank you" response. He looked at me and said, "I miss being in love." I was startled by the candor of his answer. When I got home I looked up his bio online. His wife of many years had passed away recently. His response when I asked that question made me ask myself, "Do I miss being in love?" No, not actively, until I ask that question, then I must admit poems of love do stir my heart. Always have. I guess that never gets old.

I am writing here about romantic love. Of course, I have lots of love in my life—from my family, my friends, and even my dog. I've always had dogs, and as soon as I saw the picture of the dog I have now, I said, "That's my dog." Her breeder had named her Kerri, and I realized that her name just coincidentally happened to

15

be my first stage name when I was in a nightclub chorus line. I had named myself Kerri Flynn. My mother named me Edna after her mother, but I didn't love the sound of *Ed-na* as opposed to Lorelei or Gloria, so when I was modeling I just used Edna Rae, and then when I got my part in the play *Fair Game* they said Edna Rae didn't sound finished, and when I told them my whole name—Edna Rae Gillooly—they said, "We can't put that on a marquee—they'll laugh you out of the theater!" So I played around with an *E* to keep the initials and changed Edna to Ellen and Rae to McRae. I worked with that name for a few years, and when I married my third husband, Neil, I took his name and became Ellen Burstyn.

Millay had burst onto the poetry scene with this next long poem, "Renascence." (By the way, the title "Renascence" means *renaissance*. I'm not sure why Millay chose that eccentric spelling, but that is how you pronounce it, "Ren-ay-scence.") She was called the greatest woman poet since Sappho of ancient Greece. And she was a leader in that arena until her death in 1950.

Renascence

Edna St. Vincent Millay

All I could see from where I stood
Was three long mountains and a wood;
I turned and looked another way,
And saw three islands in a bay.
So with my eyes I traced the line
Of the horizon, thin and fine,
Straight around till I was come
Back to where I'd started from;
And all I saw from where I stood
Was three long mountains and a wood.

Over these things I could not see:
These were the things that bounded me.
And I could touch them with my hand,
Almost, I thought, from where I stand!
And all at once things seemed so small
My breath came short, and scarce at all.

But, sure, the sky is big, I said:
Miles and miles above my head.
So here upon my back I'll lie
And look my fill into the sky.
And so I looked, and after all,

The sky was not so very tall.
The sky, I said, must somewhere stop . . .
And—sure enough!—I see the top!
The sky, I thought, is not so grand;
I 'most could touch it with my hand!
And reaching up my hand to try,
I screamed, to feel it touch the sky.

I screamed, and—lo!—Infinity
Came down and settled over me;
Forced back my scream into my chest;
Bent back my arm upon my breast;
And, pressing of the Undefined
The definition on my mind,
Held up before my eyes a glass
Through which my shrinking sight did pass
Until it seemed I must behold
Immensity made manifold;
Whispered to me a word whose sound
Deafened the air for worlds around,
And brought unmuffled to my ears
The gossiping of friendly spheres,
The creaking of the tented sky,
The ticking of Eternity.

I saw and heard, and knew at last
The How and Why of all things, past,
And present, and forevermore.
The Universe, cleft to the core,
Lay open to my probing sense,
That, sickening, I would fain pluck thence
But could not,—nay! but needs must suck
At the great wound, and could not pluck
My lips away till I had drawn
All venom out.—Ah, fearful pawn:
For my omniscience paid I toll
In infinite remorse of soul.

All sin was of my sinning, all
Atoning mine, and mine the gall
Of all regret. Mine was the weight
Of every brooded wrong, the hate
That stood behind each envious thrust,
Mine every greed, mine every lust.

And all the while, for every grief,
Each suffering, I craved relief
With individual desire;
Craved all in vain! And felt fierce fire
About a thousand people crawl;
Perished with each,—then mourned for all!

A man was starving in Capri;
He moved his eyes and looked at me;
I felt his gaze, I heard his moan,
And knew his hunger as my own.
I saw at sea a great fog bank
Between two ships that struck and sank;
A thousand screams the heavens smote;
And every scream tore through my throat.

No hurt I did not feel, no death
That was not mine; mine each last breath
That, crying, met an answering cry
From the compassion that was I.
All suffering mine, and mine its rod;
Mine, pity like the pity of God.

Ah, awful weight! Infinity
Pressed down upon the finite Me!
My anguished spirit, like a bird,
Beating against my lips I heard;
Yet lay the weight so close about
There was no room for it without.
And so beneath the weight lay I
And suffered death, but could not die.

Long had I lain thus, craving death,
When quietly the earth beneath
Gave way, and inch by inch, so great
At last had grown the crushing weight,
Into the earth I sank till I
Full six feet under ground did lie,
And sank no more,—there is no weight
Can follow here, however great.
From off my breast I felt it roll,
And as it went my tortured soul
Burst forth and fled in such a gust
That all about me swirled the dust.

Deep in the earth I rested now.
Cool is its hand upon the brow
And soft its breast beneath the head
Of one who is so gladly dead.
And all at once, and over all
The pitying rain began to fall;
I lay and heard each pattering hoof
Upon my lowly, thatchèd roof,
And seemed to love the sound far more
Than ever I had done before.
For rain it hath a friendly sound
To one who's six feet under ground;
And scarce the friendly voice or face,
A grave is such a quiet place.

The rain, I said, is kind to come
And speak to me in my new home.
I would I were alive again
To kiss the fingers of the rain,
To drink into my eyes the shine
Of every slanting silver line,
To catch the freshened, fragrant breeze
From drenched and dripping apple-trees.
For soon the shower will be done,
And then the broad face of the sun
Will laugh above the rain-soaked earth
Until the world with answering mirth
Shakes joyously, and each round drop
Rolls, twinkling, from its grass-blade top.

How can I bear it, buried here,
While overhead the sky grows clear
And blue again after the storm?
O, multi-coloured, multi-form,
Belovèd beauty over me,
That I shall never, never see
Again! Spring-silver, autumn-gold,
That I shall never more behold!—
Sleeping your myriad magics through,
Close-sepulchred away from you!
O God, I cried, give me new birth,

And put me back upon the earth!
Upset each cloud's gigantic gourd
And let the heavy rain, down-poured
In one big torrent, set me free,
Washing my grave away from me!

I ceased; and through the breathless hush
That answered me, the far-off rush
Of herald wings came whispering
Like music down the vibrant string
Of my ascending prayer, and—crash!
Before the wild wind's whistling lash
The startled storm-clouds reared on high
And plunged in terror down the sky!
And the big rain in one black wave
Fell from the sky and struck my grave.

I know not how such things can be;
I only know there came to me
A fragrance such as never clings
To aught save happy living things;
A sound as of some joyous elf
Singing sweet songs to please himself,
And, through and over everything,
A sense of glad awakening.
The grass, a-tiptoe at my ear,

Whispering to me I could hear;
I felt the rain's cool finger-tips
Brushed tenderly across my lips,
Laid gently on my sealèd sight,
And all at once the heavy night
Fell from my eyes and I could see!—
A drenched and dripping apple-tree,
A last long line of silver rain,
A sky grown clear and blue again.
And as I looked a quickening gust
Of wind blew up to me and thrust
Into my face a miracle
Of orchard-breath, and with the smell,—
I know not how such things can be!—
I breathed my soul back into me.

Ah! Up then from the ground sprang I
And hailed the earth with such a cry
As is not heard save from a man
Who has been dead, and lives again.
About the trees my arms I wound;
Like one gone mad I hugged the ground;
I raised my quivering arms on high;
I laughed and laughed into the sky;
Till at my throat a strangling sob
Caught fiercely, and a great heart-throb

Sent instant tears into my eyes:
O God, I cried, no dark disguise
Can e'er hereafter hide from me
Thy radiant identity!

Thou canst not move across the grass
But my quick eyes will see Thee pass,
Nor speak, however silently,
But my hushed voice will answer Thee.
I know the path that tells Thy way
Through the cool eve of every day;
God, I can push the grass apart
And lay my finger on Thy heart!

The world stands out on either side
No wider than the heart is wide;
Above the world is stretched the sky,—
No higher than the soul is high.
The heart can push the sea and land
Farther away on either hand;
The soul can split the sky in two,
And let the face of God shine through.
But East and West will pinch the heart
That can not keep them pushed apart;
And he whose soul is flat—the sky
Will cave in on him by and by.

I read this poem when I was quite young, about twenty years old. It was the first time I read a poem about a spiritually transformative experience. I had only been away from my mother's house for two years at the most. I was working as a model in the J. L. Hudson Company, a big department store in downtown Detroit. I didn't yet know about spiritual concepts other than what I had been taught in my Catholic boarding school, and yet when I read this poem it spoke to me about a dimension of life that I knew nothing about—the transformative experience—and it awakened something in me.

When she said that "the world stands out on either side / No wider than the heart is wide," it planted a seed in me. I wanted to be that. I wanted to walk through the world with a heart that wide, whatever that meant. I wasn't sure. But I carried that seed and did my best to be nourished by whatever grew from it. Don't get me wrong, it's not like I was a virtuous girl. I was a bit of a tramp. I experienced being wanted, and I am afraid he who wanted me pretty much got me. I was so pleased at last to feel wanted. It took me some learning as well as some living to . . . as the poets say, "wake up."

This next poem, "Love is not all," I consider one of her greatest and certainly one of my favorites:

Love is not all: it is not meat nor drink
Edna St. Vincent Millay

Love is not all: it is not meat nor drink
Nor slumber nor a roof against the rain;
Nor yet a floating spar to men that sink
And rise and sink and rise and sink again;
Love can not fill the thickened lung with breath,
Nor clean the blood, nor set the fractured bone;
Yet many a man is making friends with death
Even as I speak, for lack of love alone.
It well may be that in a difficult hour,
Pinned down by pain and moaning for release,
Or nagged by want past resolution's power,
I might be driven to sell your love for peace,
Or trade the memory of this night for food.
It well may be. I do not think I would.

I had treasured this poem, and years later I was attending a fund-raiser for the Millay Colony for the Arts (now called Milly Arts), run by Edna's sister Norma, and the poem was recited brilliantly by the great actor Roscoe Lee Browne. Roscoe was a member of the Actors Studio, as I was by then, but we didn't know each other.

Nor did we know of our mutual love for poetry, especially Millay's. But we talked and became friends. He visited my apartment in New York, and we shared our favorite poems.

In the late 1960s and early 1970s I was living with my husband in Hollywood. When I say Hollywood, it communicates moviemaking glamour, Tinseltown. But really it is just a neighborhood in Los Angeles with streets lined with nice middle-class homes. I lived in the Hollywood Hills, in a lovely duplex apartment with a working fireplace. I was established in the business by then, doing guest shots on TV shows. I made a comfortable income. I attended the Actors Studio's acting sessions whenever Lee Strasberg was in Los Angeles and moderating the sessions. I had studied with him in New York and was very happy when he began to spend his summers in LA, when the Actors Studio in New York was closed for the summer.

I ran into Roscoe there and invited him to visit me at home so we could carry on our poetry-swapping visits that we had begun in New York. We would sit on the floor in my living room and say some version of "How 'bout this one?"

Roscoe knew many poems by heart because beside his successful career as an actor and a director, he also had done a tour reciting poetry with an actor named Anthony Zerbe. Roscoe knew many more poems than I did and had such a beautiful sonorous voice. I was in heaven listening to him.

I didn't know, when I attended that fundraiser for the Millay Colony, that Norma was working on organizing her sister Edna's papers with the help of an assistant named Mary Oliver, who has stated that she was very influenced by the work of Edna St. Vincent Millay.

Mary Oliver went on to win the Pulitzer Prize for Poetry in 1984, which had also been won by Millay, who was the first woman in history to win it, in 1923. Oliver has described her home life as dysfunctional. Her poem "The Journey" describes her leaving her home, just as it does my own leaving, when I was a teenager.

The Journey
Mary Oliver

One day you finally knew
what you had to do, and began,
though the voices around you
kept shouting
their bad advice—
though the whole house
began to tremble
and you felt the old tug
at your ankles.
"Mend my life!"
each voice cried.
But you didn't stop.
You knew what you had to do,
though the wind pried

with its stiff fingers
at the very foundations—
though their melancholy
was terrible.
It was already late
enough, and a wild night,
and the road full of fallen
branches and stones.
But little by little,
as you left their voices behind,
the stars began to burn
through the sheets of clouds,
and there was a new voice,
which you slowly
recognized as your own,
that kept you company
as you strode deeper and deeper
into the world,
determined to do
the only thing you could do—
determined to save
the only life you could save.

Speaking of love . . . as I mentioned, I have been married three times. I married my first husband, Bill Alexander, when I was nineteen. He sold cars for a living, but he had previously owned a bookstore and he was a poet; not a published poet, but nonetheless, he wrote poems. I only remember one of them:

My uncle stands sniffing a paper rose.
If this be madness, what of charm?

Bill was the one who started me on collecting fine books, a hobby for many years, one that I'll never give up. I treasure my fine library.

I learned so much from Bill about literature and especially poetry.

One of Bill's favorite poets was Charles Baudelaire, and he introduced me to his strangely beautiful poetry.

I memorized this poem during the period I was married to Bill, in Detroit in the 1950s. I lost track of the edition of his collection of Baudelaire through our divorce, and I wanted to use that particular translator's version, but I couldn't remember his name. But because I memorized one of his poems, I was able to track down the translator, whose name is Lewis Piaget Shanks, by reciting the poem into my iPad. Isn't it amazing that our minds tuck away something we memorized seventy-something years ago, and we can call it forth after all that time?

When I was in Paris earlier last year, I had hoped Baudelaire's home was still standing and had become a museum I could visit. But when I inquired about that, I learned about the modernization of Paris by Baron Georges-Eugène Haussmann at the direction of Napoleon III beginning in the 1850s. That's when Paris became the open city with its wide boulevards instead of the narrow streets of Baudelaire's time. Baudelaire's house was long gone.

This is Lewis Piaget Shanks's translation, which Bill favored:

The Death of Lovers
Charles Baudelaire

beds of subtle fragrance shall be ours,
soft divans far deeper than a tomb,
fairer climes shall yield mysterious flowers
—flowers which for us were made to bloom.

lavishing our final amorous hours
there, our flaming hearts shall merge and loom
in the twin mirrors of these souls of ours
—torches vast which side by side consume.

then some evening, rose and mystic blue,
charged with the sobbing woe of our adieu,
Love shall link us in one lightning-spark;

later, shall the faithful angel fling
all the portals wide, illumining
the flameless torches and the mirrors dark.

TRANSLATED BY LEWIS PIAGET SHANKS

I have always been grateful to Bill for all he taught me. But the marriage didn't last for more than five years! I had left Detroit and gotten established as a model and started doing commercials in New York City when I went back to Detroit for a visit. We got together and shortly afterward we got married. So, I abandoned my budding career and moved back to where I came from.

One day I went shopping in the J. L. Hudson department store, where I had worked before, and they had a sale on B. H. Wragge clothes, one of my favorite designers at the time. The dresses were marked way down so I bought a few at the very reduced price. When the bill came, my husband Bill said, "I can't pay for your clothes." I just stared at him. I had no money. I wasn't sure what to say. Finally, I said, "What do we do?" He said, "You've got to go to work." So, I called my old modeling agency and went back to work as a model. When a check came from the agency, Bill was furious. When I reminded him that he said I had to work, I didn't understand. He exploded and said, "Well, I didn't tell you to go out and bring home more money than I earn." He was *furious*.

It was my first glaring example of the unspoken rule of the patriarchy. The woman must be less than. She must be shorter in height and less than in every other way possible. And she was certainly not to bring home higher earnings than the man. Our marriage just dwindled after that.

But in the future that absolute patriarchy would begin to change, like in the 1960s when May Sarton wrote this poem:

New Year Poem
May Sarton

> Let us step outside for a moment
> As the sun breaks through clouds
> And shines on wet new fallen snow,
> And breathe the new air.
> So much has died that had to die this year.
>
> We are dying away from things.
> It is a necessity—we have to do it
> Or we shall be buried under the magazines,
> The too many clothes, the too much food.
> We have dragged it all around

Like dung beetles
Who drag piles of dung
Behind them on which to feed,
In which to lay their eggs.

Let us step outside for a moment
Among ocean, clouds, a white field,
Islands floating in the distance.
They have always been there.
But we have not been there.

We are going to drive slowly
And see the small poor farms,
The lovely shape of leafless trees
Their shadows blue on the snow.
We are going to learn the sharp edge
Of perception after a day's fast.

There is nothing to fear.
About this revolution . . .
Though it will change our minds.
Aggression, violence, machismo
Are fading from us
Like old photographs
Faintly ridiculous
(Did a man actually step like a goose

To instill fear?
Does a boy have to kill
To become a man?)

Already there are signs.
Young people plant gardens.
Fathers change their babies' diapers
And are learning to cook.

Let us step outside for a moment.
It is all there
Only we have been slow to arrive
At a way of seeing it.
Unless the gentle inherit the earth
There will be no earth.

Bill started not coming home right after work and going to the bar instead. One night I saw myself sitting at home waiting for him with a glass of Jack Daniels in my hand and I thought, *This is what I gave up my career for?* I moved back to New York and resumed my career. Bill was supposed to follow me, and we talked on the phone regularly about his coming, but he never came. He probably never intended to. When I got the lead in my first play—it was called *Fair Game*—I took a plane to Mexico for the divorce, and the next day I went into the first day of rehearsal a single woman.

But I carried with me all the poetry that Bill had exposed me to, and for that I am forever grateful. This Millay poem, "Souvenir," comes to mind. The memory of what once was, after it is all over.

Souvenir
Edna St. Vincent Millay

> Just a rainy day or two
> In a windy tower,
> That was all I had of you—
> Saving half an hour.
>
> Marred by greeting passing groups
> In a cinder walk,
> Near some naked blackberry hoops
> Dim with purple chalk.
>
> I remember three or four
> Things you said in spite,
> And an ugly coat you wore,
> Plaided black and white.
>
> Just a rainy day or two
> And a bitter word.
> Why do I remember you
> As a singing bird?

Those last lines "Why do I remember you / As a singing bird?" Oh, the longing in that line for what is over and yet remembered so fondly. It would take another ten years or so before the change started to happen, to when I began to remember him that way.

𝒥

Bill was the one who made me truly love Poe, even though I was introduced to him in high school, and the musicality and the meter of his poetry made it so easy to memorize. Edgar Allan Poe was known as a poet but also a short story writer. His book of short stories called *Tales of Mystery and Imagination* is considered to be the inspiration for the mystery/detective story—he created that genre.

Baudelaire read Edgar Allan Poe in English. He felt there was a kinship of a kind in their writing, and even though his English was hardly perfect, he began having his translations of Poe published in Paris. Consequently, Poe became famous in France before he was very well-known in America. And the more Baudelaire translated Poe, the better his English became. He translated Poe's short stories as well as the poems. And it's how the mystery story genre was started in France.

I love Poe's stories, but I love his poetry even more. They all carry a feeling of some kind to the reader.

I memorized this next poem when I was in my twenties, and it's still with me after all these years. Most rhyme schemes end at the end of a sentence, as with the first verse with see/Lee/me, but I do love in the fifth verse the inner rhyme of "ever dissever." And the word *sea* is used in every verse like the sound of the sea crashing on the shore of your mind. This poem is considered a perfect example of a metrical poem, meaning it has meter or rhythm and a definite rhyme scheme. All metrical poems do. (If you listen to my recording of "Annabel Lee," you can hear the meter.) Later we will get to poems that don't have that rhyme scheme—they're called blank verse and also free verse.

"Annabel Lee" is a sad poem about the loss of a beautiful young girl. We know that Poe's mother and stepmother died young and then he married his beautiful cousin who also died when she was still very young, so the loss of a beloved and beautiful love became the focus of this poem. It is sad, but it is also beautifully sad.

Recently, I shared a line of the Iranian American poet Kaveh Akbar whom I met at Poetry House in New York City. He wrote this extraordinary line: "Art is where what we survive survives." Poe survived the deaths of his mother and his stepmother at a young age and then the death of his young beautiful wife. I think you don't really know who you are until you experience grief. All that grief survives here as his art.

Annabel Lee
Edgar Allan Poe

It was many and many a year ago,
　　In a kingdom by the sea,
That a maiden there lived whom you may know
　　By the name of Annabel Lee;
And this maiden she lived with no other thought
　　Than to love and be loved by me.

I was a child and *she* was a child,
　　In this kingdom by the sea,
But we loved with a love that was more than love—
　　I and my Annabel Lee—
With a love that the wingèd seraphs of Heaven
　　Coveted her and me.

And this was the reason that, long ago,
　　In this kingdom by the sea,
A wind blew out of a cloud, chilling
　　My beautiful Annabel Lee;
So that her highborn kinsman came
　　And bore her away from me,
To shut her up in a sepulchre
　　In this kingdom by the sea.

The angels, not half so happy in Heaven,
    Went envying her and me—
Yes!—that was the reason (as all men know,
    In this kingdom by the sea)
That the wind came out of the cloud by night,
    Chilling and killing my Annabel Lee.

But our love it was stronger by far than the love
    Of those who were older than we—
    Of many far wiser than we—
And neither the angels in Heaven above,
    Nor the demons down under the sea,
Can ever dissever my soul from the soul
    Of the beautiful Annabel Lee;

For the moon never beams, without bringing me dreams
    Of the beautiful Annabel Lee;
And the stars never rise but I feel the bright eyes
    Of the beautiful Annabel Lee;
And so, all the night-tide, I lie down by the side
    Of my darling—my darling—my life and my bride,
    In her sepulchre there by the sea—
    In her tomb by the sounding sea.

This pen-and-ink drawing of Edgar Allan Poe was created
by a friend of my husband Bill and hung in our home while
we lived together. I inherited it in the divorce and lived with
it for years. It now hangs in my son Jefferson's home.

A perfect example of poetry being the music of language is "The Bells" by Edgar Allan Poe. The rhythm of it, the musicality . . . this is a poem that begs to be read out loud. You can hear the tolling of the bells. I was amazed at his use of language, which is just sheer music. Read it out loud and enjoy the music of the language.

The Bells
Edgar Allan Poe

I.

         Hear the sledges with the bells—
            Silver bells!
What a world of merriment their melody foretells!
         How they tinkle, tinkle, tinkle,
         In the icy air of night!
            While the stars that oversprinkle
            All the Heavens, seem to twinkle
         With a crystalline delight;
            Keeping time, time, time,
            In a sort of Runic rhyme,
         To the tintinnabulation that so musically wells
         From the bells, bells, bells, bells,
         Bells, bells, bells—
          From the jingling and the tinkling of the bells.

II.

Hear the mellow wedding bells—
　　Golden bells!
What a world of happiness their harmony foretells!
　　Through the balmy air of night
　　How they ring out their delight!—
　　　From the molten-golden notes,
　　　　And all in time,
　　　What a liquid ditty floats
　　To the turtle-dove that listens, while she gloats
　　　On the moon!
　　Oh, from out the sounding cells,
What a gush of euphony voluminously wells!
　　　How it swells!
　　　How it dwells
　　On the future!—how it tells
　　Of the rapture that impels
　　To the swinging and the ringing
　　Of the bells, bells, bells—
　　Of the bells, bells, bells, bells,
　　　Bells, bells, bells—
　　To the rhyming and the chiming of the bells!

III.

Hear the loud alarum bells—
　　Brazen bells!

44

What a tale of terror, now, their turbulency tells!
  In the startled ear of Night
  How they scream out their affright!
   Too much horrified to speak,
   They can only shriek, shriek,
       Out of tune,
In a clamorous appealing to the mercy of the fire,
In a mad expostulation with the deaf and frantic fire
      Leaping higher, higher, higher,
       With a desperate desire,
       And a resolute endeavour
       Now—now to sit, or never,
    By the side of the pale-faced moon.
      Oh, the bells, bells, bells!
       What a tale their terror tells
         Of despair!
    How they clang, and clash, and roar!
    What a horror they outpour
On the bosom of the palpitating air!
   Yet the ear, it fully knows,
       By the twanging,
       And the clanging,
    How the danger ebbs and flows;
   Yes, the ear distinctly tells,
       In the jangling,
       And the wrangling,

How the danger sinks and swells,
By the sinking or the swelling in the anger of the bells—
Of the bells—
Of the bells, bells, bells, bells,
Bells, bells, bells—
In the clamor and the clangor of the bells!

IV.

Hear the tolling of the bells—
Iron bells!
What a world of solemn thought their monody compels!
In the silence of the night,
How we shiver with affright
At the melancholy menace of their tone!
For every sound that floats
From the rust within their throats
Is a groan.
And the people—ah, the people—
They that dwell up in the steeple,
All alone,
And who, tolling, tolling, tolling,
In that muffled monotone,
Feel a glory in so rolling
On the human heart a stone—
They are neither man nor woman—
They are neither brute nor human—

They are Ghouls:—
And their king it is who tolls:—
And he rolls, rolls, rolls,
    Rolls
  A Pæan from the bells!
And his merry bosom swells
  With the Pæan of the bells!
And he dances and he yells;
Keeping time, time, time,
In a sort of Runic rhyme,
  To the Pæan of the bells—
  Of the bells:—
Keeping time, time, time,
In a sort of Runic rhyme,
  To the throbbing of the bells—
Of the bells, bells, bells—
  To the sobbing of the bells:—
Keeping time, time, time,
  As he knells, knells, knells,
In a happy Runic rhyme,
  To the rolling of the bells—
Of the bells, bells, bells:—
  To the tolling of the bells—
Of the bells, bells, bells, bells,
  Bells, bells, bells—
To the moaning and the groaning of the bells.

And here is Poe's most famous poem:

The Raven
Edgar Allan Poe

Once upon a midnight dreary, while I pondered, weak and
    weary,
Over many a quaint and curious volume of forgotten lore—
    While I nodded, nearly napping, suddenly there came a
       tapping,
As of some one gently rapping, rapping at my chamber door.
"'Tis some visitor," I muttered, "tapping at my chamber
    door—
       Only this and nothing more."

Ah, distinctly I remember it was in the bleak December;
And each separate dying ember wrought its ghost upon the
    floor.
    Eagerly I wished the morrow;—vainly I had sought to
     borrow
    From my books surcease of sorrow—sorrow for the lost
      Lenore—
For the rare and radiant maiden whom the angels name
     Lenore—
    Nameless *here* for evermore.

And the silken, sad, uncertain rustling of each purple
    curtain
Thrilled me—filled me with fantastic terrors never felt
    before;
    So that now, to still the beating of my heart, I stood
        repeating
    "'Tis some visitor entreating entrance at my chamber
        door—
Some late visitor entreating entrance at my chamber door;—
        This it is and nothing more."

    Presently my soul grew stronger; hesitating then no
        longer,
"Sir," said I, "or Madam, truly your forgiveness I implore;
    But the fact is I was napping, and so gently you came
        rapping,
    And so faintly you came tapping, tapping at my
        chamber door,
That I scarce was sure I heard you"—here I opened wide the
    door;—
        Darkness there and nothing more.

    Deep into that darkness peering, long I stood there
        wondering, fearing,
Doubting, dreaming dreams no mortal ever dared to dream
    before;

But the silence was unbroken, and the stillness gave no
   token,
And the only word there spoken was the whispered
   word, "Lenore?"
This I whispered, and an echo murmured back the word,
   "Lenore!"—
     Merely this and nothing more.

Back into the chamber turning, all my soul within me
   burning,
Soon again I heard a tapping somewhat louder than before.
  "Surely," said I, "surely that is something at my window
    lattice;
  Let me see, then, what thereat is, and this mystery
    explore—
Let my heart be still a moment and this mystery explore;—
    'Tis the wind and nothing more!"

Open here I flung the shutter, when, with many a flirt
   and flutter,
In there stepped a stately Raven of the saintly days of yore;
  Not the least obeisance made he; not a minute stopped
    or stayed he;
  But, with mien of lord or lady, perched above my
    chamber door—

Perched upon a bust of Pallas just above my chamber
    door—
        Perched, and sat, and nothing more.

Then this ebony bird beguiling my sad fancy into smiling,
By the grave and stern decorum of the countenance it wore,
"Though thy crest be shorn and shaven, thou," I said, "art
    sure no craven,
Ghastly grim and ancient Raven wandering from the
    Nightly shore—
Tell me what thy lordly name is on the Night's Plutonian
    shore!"
        Quoth the Raven "Nevermore."

Much I marvelled this ungainly fowl to hear discourse
    so plainly,
Though its answer little meaning—little relevancy bore;
  For we cannot help agreeing that no living human being
  Ever yet was blessed with seeing bird above his
    chamber door—
Bird or beast upon the sculptured bust above his chamber
    door,
      With such name as "Nevermore."

  But the Raven, sitting lonely on the placid bust, spoke
    only

That one word, as if his soul in that one word he did
    outpour.
    Nothing farther then he uttered—not a feather then he
        fluttered—
    Till I scarcely more than muttered "Other friends have
        flown before—
On the morrow *he* will leave me, as my Hopes have flown
    before."
        Then the bird said "Nevermore."

Startled at the stillness broken by reply so aptly spoken,
"Doubtless," said I, "what it utters is its only stock and store
    Caught from some unhappy master whom unmerciful
        Disaster
    Followed fast and followed faster till his songs one
        burden bore—
Till the dirges of his Hope that melancholy burden bore
        Of 'Never—nevermore'."

But the Raven still beguiling all my fancy into smiling,
Straight I wheeled a cushioned seat in front of bird, and bust
    and door;
    Then, upon the velvet sinking, I betook myself to
        linking
    Fancy unto fancy, thinking what this ominous bird of
        yore—

What this grim, ungainly, ghastly, gaunt, and ominous bird
of yore
Meant in croaking "Nevermore."

This I sat engaged in guessing, but no syllable
expressing
To the fowl whose fiery eyes now burned into my bosom's
core;
This and more I sat divining, with my head at ease
reclining
On the cushion's velvet lining that the lamp-light
gloated o'er,
But whose velvet-violet lining with the lamp-light
gloating o'er,
She shall press, ah, nevermore!

Then, methought, the air grew denser, perfumed
from an unseen censer
Swung by Seraphim whose foot-falls tinkled on the tufted
floor.
"Wretch," I cried, "thy God hath lent thee—by these
angels he hath sent thee
Respite—respite and nepenthe from thy memories of
Lenore;
Quaff, oh quaff this kind nepenthe and forget this lost
Lenore!"
Quoth the Raven "Nevermore."

"Prophet!" said I, "thing of evil!—prophet still, if bird
    or devil!—
Whether Tempter sent, or whether tempest tossed thee here
    ashore,
    Desolate yet all undaunted, on this desert land
        enchanted—
    On this home by Horror haunted—tell me truly, I
        implore—
Is there—*is* there balm in Gilead?—tell me—tell me, I
    implore!"
                Quoth the Raven "Nevermore."

"Prophet!" said I, "thing of evil!—prophet still, if bird
    or devil!
By that Heaven that bends above us—by that God we both
    adore—
    Tell this soul with sorrow laden if, within the distant
        Aidenn,
    It shall clasp a sainted maiden whom the angels name
        Lenore—
Clasp a rare and radiant maiden whom the angels name
    Lenore."
                Quoth the Raven "Nevermore."

"Be that word our sign of parting, bird or fiend!" I
    shrieked, upstarting—
"Get thee back into the tempest and the Night's Plutonian
    shore!
    Leave no black plume as a token of that lie thy soul hath
        spoken!
    Leave my loneliness unbroken!—quit the bust above
        my door!
Take thy beak from out my heart, and take thy form from off
    my door!"
           Quoth the Raven "Nevermore."

And the Raven, never flitting, still is sitting, *still* is
    sitting
On the pallid bust of Pallas just above my chamber door;
    And his eyes have all the seeming of a demon's that is
        dreaming,
    And the lamp-light o'er him streaming throws his
        shadow on the floor;
And my soul from out that shadow that lies floating on the
    floor
           Shall be lifted—nevermore!

𝓍

Like Poe, I didn't exactly grow up surrounded by love. Oh, I know my mother loved me, but her third husband, it seems, hated the two stepchildren he was forced to live with. And the reason for that—let me just say, knowing my mother and how she operated—was when she left her second husband, she put me and my brother in boarding school until she got husband number three, married him, and had his baby. She then told him she had two children in boarding school and brought us home to live with them. And, of course, he resented us. He was a very good father to his own son, which I was happy to see. But, you know, he looked at me when I was fourteen and said, "You'll never amount to anything."

So I was eager to leave home. I packed up on my eighteenth birthday when I was legally old enough to get out of my mother's "jurisdiction," as she called it, and walked out to freedom. I hadn't discovered yet the poetry of Mary Oliver. That came years later. But when I finally did read her poetry, I recognized her, recognized someone who had traveled the path I traveled and had come to a clearing where her song could be sung.

I set out to find my path, whatever that might be.

I earned a living modeling and thought I was heading toward acting, but it was a circuitous route. The poems I carried with me were really much closer to prayers. Here's one I traveled with. It's by the poet Thomas Merton, who was also a Trappist monk, theologian, writer, and social activist:

I Have No Idea Where I Am Going

Thomas Merton

My Lord God, I have no idea where I am going. I do not see
the road ahead of me. I cannot know for certain where it will
end. Nor do I really know myself, and the fact that I think I am
following your will does not mean that I am actually doing so.
But I believe that the desire to please you does in fact please you.
And I hope I have that desire in all that I am doing. I hope that I
will never do anything apart from that desire. And I know that if
I do this you will lead me by the right road, though I may know
nothing about it. Therefore I will trust you always though I may
seem to be lost and in the shadow of death. I will not fear, for you
are ever with me, and you will never leave me to face my perils
alone.

"I have no idea where I am going." That was true then, and that is true now. I do not see the road ahead of me. How can we ever see the road? We can only see the road we are on now, and see where it seems to be leading, but that doesn't mean I'll stay on this road. Surprising things happen that put you on another road in a blink of an eye. All of that first verse seems to be true, but it's the second verse that lands in me. Lands somewhere in the heart area:

"But I believe that the desire to please you does in fact please you."

That's the sentence that makes me hear a yes in my general heart area. But why? Do I know who the "you" is that I have a desire to please? One assumes it's God, but do I believe in God? Yes, but on the other hand, no. Not God as the church promotes: the super patriarch that we bow to. I'm not sure if God is a being, a consciousness, or a process. I just know that I do believe there is another dimension to life that we are aware of in our hearts when we choose to be. And that entity, in whatever form it manifests, is something I like to please. Not because if I don't please this divinity, I will be in danger of being sent to hell, but because I know that what pleases this presence is virtue, integrity, right mindedness, and right actions and kindness. Which reminds me that in the language of Jesus, Aramaic, instead of "good" and "bad" those words are translated as "ripe" and "not ripe." I like that. So, what makes this celestial being smile in approval of my actions is whether or not they're ripe. Or in other words . . . conscious.

ℐ

I had some little containers I called my *poetry packs*. I don't remember where I got them I have had them for so long. They are made out of some kind of basket material, woven into little packages that fit into one another. I had my favorite poems typed on colored note cards and kept them inside the poetry packs. They are light and flat, so easy to carry. I think of them as my antidote to boredom. If I ever got caught in a dentist's waiting room or a train station, I pulled out my poetry pack and selected one to memorize as I sat there. But I don't need to do that anymore as I've memorized so many poems. I carry my own packet inside my head and my heart.

I believe it doesn't really matter if you believe in the old-man-on-a-throne-in-heaven concept, or if you believe in an everywhere-present consciousness, or a blessed everything, or a creative intelligence, or one god, or many gods.

Ooh, that's from a poem by David Whyte, wait a minute. I have to look for it. I never memorized it.

I was just writing that it doesn't matter which version of divinity you use as a model of the divine creator as long as you have some version of the, let's say, ultimate guiding force that you desire to please—just in case you ever falter and feel your feet sliding off the path into territory that has no place in your credo. Sorry, don't mean to preach here, but it is so easy to slide off that path.

Oh, I just found that poem of David Whyte's that got triggered when I was writing. Here it is:

Self-Portrait

David Whyte

It doesn't interest me if there is one God
or many gods.
I want to know if you belong or feel
abandoned,
if you know despair or see it in others.
I want to know
if you are prepared to live in the world
with its harsh need
to change you. If you can look back
with firm eyes,
saying this is where I stand. I want to know
if you know
how to melt into that fierce heat of living,
falling toward
the center of your longing. I want to know
if you are willing
to live, day by day, with the consequence of love
and the bitter
unwanted passion of your sure defeat.

I have heard, in *that* fierce embrace, even
the gods speak of God.

ℐ

This poem by Portia Nelson called "Autobiography in Five Short Chapters" describes perfectly my learning process as I stumbled through those early days on my own.

Autobiography in Five Short Chapters
Portia Nelson

Chapter One

I walk down the street.
There is a deep hole in the sidewalk.
I fall in.
I am lost . . . . I am helpless.
It isn't my fault.
It takes forever to find a way out.

Chapter Two

I walk down the same street.
There is a deep hole in the sidewalk.
I pretend I don't see it.
I fall in again.
I can't believe I am in this same place.
But, it isn't my fault.
It still takes a long time to get out.

Chapter Three

I walk down the same street.
   There is a deep hole in the sidewalk.
   I see it is there.
   I still fall in . . . it's a habit . . . but,
      my eyes are open.
      I know where I am.
It is *my* fault.
I get out immediately.

Chapter Four

I walk down the same street.
   There is a deep hole in the sidewalk.
   I walk around it.

Chapter Five

I walk down another street.

For me this poem is really about learning a method for living consciously. It's addressing our habits that keep us making the same mistakes in our lives over and over. Wrong food, cigarettes, alcohol—all habits I've learned to "walk down another street." It's amazing how often letting go of a habit brings about a profound change. It's not always easy to change a habit, but we have to find a method that works for us. I discovered one of my more surprising techniques when I was giving up smoking cigarettes: I found that my most vulnerable time was after a meal. That's when I most craved a cigarette. I examined the feeling, and I learned that the craving wasn't so much in my lungs or my mouth, that it was in my hands. I wanted to reach for a cigarette, I wanted to light it, I wanted to blow out the match in my hand, and then bring the cigarette to my lips and inhale.

Soon after that discovery I was invited to lunch by a friend, and I knew what to anticipate at the end of the meal. I found a solution. When we finished eating, I explained I was giving up smoking, and I hoped that she would excuse me when I took out my coloring book and crayons and colored a picture as we continued our conversation.

♪

Benedictio
Edward Abbey

Benedictio: May your trails be crooked, winding, lonesome, dangerous, leading to the most amazing views. May your mountains rise into and above the clouds. May your rivers flow without end, meandering through pastoral valleys tinkling with bells, past temples and castles and poets' towers into a dark primeval forest where tigers belch and monkeys howl, through miasmal and mysterious swamps and down into a desert of red rock, blue mesas, domes and pinnacles and grottoes of endless stone, and down again into a deep vast ancient unknown chasm where bars of sunlight blaze on profiled cliffs, where deer walk across the white sand beaches, where storms come and go as lightning clangs upon the high crags, where something strange and more beautiful and more full of wonder than your deepest dreams waits for you—beyond that next turning of the canyon walls.

So long.

That poem is what I wish for any young person just starting out on their own—wish for adventure. I read somewhere some very good advice: "Don't spend your money on things, spend it on experiences." We grow up in fairly protected environments, and it's only when we move out into the world where people live differently (the more differently the better) that our minds expand into broader ways to view our own world.

I have been blessed with opportunities to visit some far-flung places. I have climbed to the top of the Great Pyramid in Egypt and viewed the sun rising over Cairo. I've tracked wild gorillas in the jungles of Rwanda and attended an outdoor music festival in Morocco, where they were playing Eastern spiritual music. Those experiences taught me how to accept the differences in people, in countries, and in religions. It taught me to be tolerant of others and, most importantly, of their belief systems.

I Wandered Lonely as a Cloud
William Wordsworth

I wandered lonely as a cloud
That floats on high o'er vales and hills,
When all at once I saw a crowd,
A host, of golden daffodils;
Beside the lake, beneath the trees,
Fluttering and dancing in the breeze.

Continuous as the stars that shine
And twinkle on the milky way,
They stretched in never-ending line
Along the margin of a bay:
Ten thousand saw I at a glance,
Tossing their heads in sprightly dance.

The waves beside them danced; but they
Out-did the sparkling waves in glee:
A poet could not but be gay,
In such a jocund company:
I gazed—and gazed—but little thought
What wealth the show to me had brought:

For oft, when on my couch I lie
In vacant or in pensive mood,
They flash upon that inward eye
Which is the bliss of solitude;
And then my heart with pleasure fills,
And dances with the daffodils.

After carrying that poem inside me for many years, I moved into a house on the Hudson River that had a beautiful view of the river and a lovely pool. But it had no flowers on the grounds. Trees? Yes, and bushes, but no flowers. So I planted a row of daffodils on the river side of the house facing the sunrise. When they were in bloom, I would sit by the water beneath the trees and enjoy them, "fluttering and dancing in the breeze." Then most often that lovely poem of Wordsworth's would speak to me.

That may be the beginning of my love of gardening. Those daffodils were planted by a house I was renting, but consequently I bought a house nearby, and then I was able to extend my love of gardening to vegetables too. I remember when I was a child during World War II, everyone was encouraged to grow their own food, if they had a yard. I have a distinct memory of sitting on the kitchen steps, eating a tomato I had just plucked from the tomato plants we were growing in our "victory garden." It was so tasty; over the years I've tried to recreate that intense tomato taste but the tomatoes I've bought in a store seem so tasteless by comparison. Finally, I learned why. It's because the flavor of the tomato is in a gene that is killed by cold. If the tomato was grown somewhere far away like California or Florida or Mexico and traveled to its destination on a bed of ice, then it arrived looking beautiful but without its flavor alive in it. Isn't that astounding?

So, I always either grow my own, or now that I live in the city, I buy them from the farmers market. I have a terrace where I grow things in pots but not tomatoes. Tomatoes in pots are a joke. Their roots are ten feet deep; that doesn't work in a pot. But sitting on my terrace among my geraniums reading poetry nourishes me in another way.

These are statues of the Buddha and the goddess. They lived together in my garden for many years. Now that I live in the city, they are outside my apartment door.

Vespers

Louise Glück

In your extended absence, you permit me
use of earth, anticipating
some return on investment. I must report
failure in my assignment, principally
regarding the tomato plants.
I think I should not be encouraged to grow
tomatoes. Or, if I am, you should withhold
the heavy rains, the cold nights that come
so often here, while other regions get
twelve weeks of summer. All this
belongs to you: on the other hand,
I planted the seeds, I watched the first shoots
like wings tearing the soil, and it was my heart
broken by the blight, the black spot so quickly
multiplying in the rows. I doubt
you have a heart, in our understanding of
that term. You who do not discriminate
between the dead and the living, who are, in consequence,
immune to foreshadowing, you may not know
how much terror we bear, the spotted leaf,
the red leaves of the maple falling
even in August, in early darkness: I am responsible
for these vines.

Louise Glück is a gardener as well as a poet. I love her tone here. She obviously seems to be addressing God, but nowhere else have I ever heard anyone register their complaints in such a politely . . . (though) irritated tone.

Matins
Louise Glück

You want to know how I spend my time?
I walk the front lawn, pretending
to be weeding. You ought to know
I'm never weeding, on my knees, pulling
clumps of clover from the flower beds: in fact
I'm looking for courage, for some evidence
my life will change, though
it takes forever, checking
each clump for the symbolic
leaf, and soon the summer is ending, already
the leaves turning, always the sick trees
going first, the dying turning
brilliant yellow, while a few dark birds perform
their curfew of music. You want to see my hands?
As empty now as at the first note.
Or was the point always
to continue without a sign?

Ooh—that last line. Could it be?

Her point was to always continue without a sign.

Rumi answers that question in a poem called "Love Dogs."

Why is Rumi—a thirteenth-century Turkish Sufi, writing in Persian and translated into English by many different translators—the bestselling poet in America? Of course, the Sufis of that period were all Muslim, and that reference point is pretty much eliminated by the translators of Rumi into English. But the wisdom shines through all the various translations, and that would account for the popularity of his poems. He is speaking directly to people about their longing for connection to spirit that is still alive in us, even though so many people have turned away from organized religion. That deep need is present and calls out to us from Rumi's poetry.

First here is Rumi's poem, and then one from Rayne O'Brian, also called "Love Dogs." No doubt inspired by Rumi.

Love Dogs

Rumi

One night a man was crying,
                    Allah! Allah!
His lips grew sweet with the praising,
until a cynic said,
                    "So! I have heard you
calling out, but have you ever
gotten any response?"

The man had no answer to that.
He quit praying and fell into a confused sleep.

He dreamed he saw Khidr, the guide of souls,
in a thick, green foliage.
                    "Why did you stop praising?"
"Because I've never heard anything back."
                            "This longing
you express *is* the return message."

The grief you cry out from
     draws you toward union.

Your pure sadness
that wants help
is the secret cup.

Listen to the moan of a dog for its master.
That whining is the connection.

There are love dogs
no one knows the names of.

Give your life
to be one of them.

TRANSLATED BY COLEMAN BARKS

Love Dogs
Rayne O'Brian

Hey. You're not gonna believe this—even I have trouble
But it happened.
I open a bank account at Wells Fargo. Okay?
The banker asks, *What's your username?*
Oh!
My feet press together in my laced school-teacher shoes.

"Lovedog," I say, keeping the moon out of my voice.
And the night orchard, and the still-warm earth
where we held each other, among the fallen apples.

A modest cough.
The banker says, *You will be*
number 3—there are two others
Two others? Three lovedogs at Wells Fargo?
I look around—is there a kennel?
The building seems to shift, Egyptian
friezes line the walls.

Where else do love dogs live?
They roam Beijing, moan in Moscow
They can change anything—turn
the Pentagon into Juilliard

Rosy tongues panting with desire
for the divine.

Three thousand years ago
the Philistines burned out Samson's eyes
Did you know that?
Sent him eyeless to Gaza—yes,
same Gaza

Rumi says:
"There are lovedogs no one knows the name of.

Give your life to be one of them."

So much work to do.

C'mon
Let's go!

What Rayne's poem would suggest is that at her bank in a suburb of San Francisco, she is the third person who is moved enough by Rumi's poem to want to use it as their identifying code name. Why was this poem so meaningful to them? Do I dare say they identify with the dog, yearning for its master? That is a metaphor for us humans, yearning for . . . "the ever present omnipotent spirit" usually referred to as "God."

I remember some time ago, I got disappointed about something. I don't remember exactly what it was; I just remember the feeling. I was expecting a certain situation to go the way I was told it was going to happen. It didn't go that way, and then I was in a state of disappointment. And I know better—expectations almost always collapse into disappointment. I forgot that, and Crash! I sat in a cloud of disappointment. But wait! I had a poem about that somewhere. I hadn't planned to use it in this book. I don't know the poet's other work. I got this poem out of an anthology and had it typed up on my special paper and put in my folder of favorite poems.

Disappointment
Tony Hoagland

> I was feeling pretty religious
> standing on the bridge in my winter coat
> looking down at the gray water:
> the sharp little waves dusted with snow,
> fish in their tin armor.
>
> That's what I like about disappointment:
> the way it slows you down,
> when the querulous insistent chatter of desire
>   goes dead calm

and the minor roadside flowers
pronounce their quiet colors,
and the red dirt of the hillside glows.

She played the flute, he played the fiddle
and the moon came up over the barn.
Then he didn't get the job,—
or her father died before she told him
        that one, most important thing—

and everything got still.

It was February or October
It was July
I remember it so clear
You don't have to pursue anything ever again
It's over
You're free
You're unemployed

You just have to stand there
looking out on the water
in your trench coat of solitude
with your scarf of resignation
                lifting in the wind.

I feel my feeling is expressed.

It's out there, on paper, for me to read.

I feel seen.

The sad feeling inside me has been shared, and expressed.

The poet's name is Tony Hoagland. Never heard of him. I look him up on Google, see his picture, read his bio. Ooh, he seems interesting. I want to read more. I order two of his books.

My disappointment of that day was eased, uplifted. . . . Lifted up into a poem if not exactly erased. . . .

At least shared.

Sharing is good.

Oh! Now, that reminds me of another poem. One by Rumi. I must share this poem of his, after what I just experienced with disappointment:

The Guest House
Rumi

> This being human is a guest house.
> Every morning a new arrival.
>
> A joy, a depression, a meanness,
> some momentary awareness comes
> as an unexpected visitor.

Welcome and entertain them all!
Even if they're a crowd of sorrows,
who violently sweep your house
empty of its furniture,
still, treat each guest honorably.
He may be clearing you out
for some new delight.

The dark thought, the shame, the malice,
meet them at the door laughing,
and invite them in.

Be grateful for whoever comes,
because each has been sent
as a guide from beyond.

TRANSLATED BY COLEMAN BARKS

That ending! "Be grateful for whoever comes, / because each has been sent / as a guide from beyond." There is no way to prove or disprove that people or events are sent to us by a guide from beyond, but it is so helpful to allow that that may be true because it changes the way we think about those people or events. It makes everything meaningful instead of living in an accidental world. It makes each arrival, be it a person or event, an opportunity for growth and an uninvited opportunity for a conscious response instead of unconscious reactivity. Always a good thing.

The Greeks believed that everyone has an inner guide. They called it a *daimon*. If you are not familiar with that word, it is pronounced *di-mon*. I believe it, because on occasion it has spoken to me in a very clear voice inside my head. So often I have had a decision to make that could be a disaster if I made the wrong choice, and then I felt a leaning, a leaning in one direction that turned out to be a remarkably right direction. But there have been a few times when I was unknowingly about to allow a disaster to be welcomed into my life, and a very clear inner voice spoke to me and instructed me, "*Stop!* Don't go there!"

I was forever grateful for that guidance.

༄

I think of myself in this period, when I was in my forties, as a searcher. I was searching for understanding, answers to questions like "What is the meaning of life?" and "Do I have a soul?" I was in a state of unknowing but wanting some understanding of what it all means. Robert Bly has translated some beautiful verses of Antonio Machado, a Spanish poet, from *Proverbs and Tiny Song*:

from *Proverbs and Tiny Songs*
Antonio Machado

2

Why should we call
these accidental furrows roads? . . .
Everyone who moves on walks
like Jesus, on the sea.

6

You walking, your footprints *are*
the road, and nothing else;
there is no road, walker,
you make the road by walking.
By walking you make the road,
and when you look backward,
you see the path that you
never will step on again.
Walker, there is no road,
only wind-trails in the sea.

7

I love Jesus, who said to us:
Heaven and earth will pass away.
When heaven and earth have passed away,

my word will still remain.
What was your word, Jesus?
Love? Forgiveness? Affection?
All your words were
one word: Wake up.

11

All things die and all things live forever;
but our task is to die,
to die making roads,
roads over the sea.

12

To die. . . . To fall like a drop
of sea water into the immense sea?
Or to be what I have never been:
one man, without shadow, without dream,
a man all alone, walking
with no road, with no mirror?

TRANSLATED BY ROBERT BLY

For years, I pondered why Machado wrote, "All your words were / one word, Wake up." Then ended the verse with two words. Only recently did I have a flash of clarity.

"It's a translation! Machado wrote in Spanish! It's probably one word in Spanish."

I look it up.

"Despierta."

It means wake up.

Duh, Ellen!

Wake up indeed.

♪

This next poet writes in Polish and was awarded the Nobel Prize in Literature in 1996. I muse so often on "The Soul." What is it? Is it real? What form does it take? Was I born with it? Did it exist before it entered my body? Is it just a story that churches made up to keep us in line? And yet, when I read a poem like this, I recognize something. Some bell is rung. It feels right.

A Few Words on the Soul

Wisława Szymborska

We have a soul at times.
No one's got it nonstop,
for keeps.

Day after day,
year after year
may pass without it.

Sometimes
it will settle for a while
only in childhood's fears and raptures.
Sometimes only in astonishment
that we are old.

It rarely lends a hand
in uphill tasks,
like moving furniture,
or lifting luggage,
or going miles in shoes that pinch.

It usually steps out
whenever meat needs chopping
or forms have to be filled.

For every thousand conversations
it participates in one,
if even that,
since it prefers silence.

Just when our body goes from ache to pain,
it slips off duty.

It's picky:
it doesn't like seeing us in crowds,
our hustling for a dubious advantage
and creaky machinations make it sick.

Joy and sorrow
aren't two different feelings for it.
It attends us
only when the two are joined.

We can count on it
when we're sure of nothing
and curious about everything.

Among the material objects
it favors clocks with pendulums
and mirrors, which keep on working
even when no one is looking.

It won't say where it comes from
or when it's taking off again,
though it's clearly expecting such questions.

We need it
but apparently
it needs us
for some reason too.

TRANSLATED BY CLARE CAVANAGH AND STANISŁAW BARAŃCZAK

There are so many things I recognize in this poem. Each verse feels right to me. I recognize in myself the things she is saying about a soul, but it is when she gets to the eighth verse—"Joy and sorrow / aren't two different feelings for it"—that suddenly something landed in me that changed my life. It happened at the Actors Studio in Los Angeles. Lee Strasberg was moderating the session. I don't remember the scene I was working on; I just remember that I cried during it. When I finished and turned to Lee for his comments, and, of course, hoping for his praise, he said, "I don't know, dear. You either laugh or you cry. If sometime you would laugh and cry at the same time, then we would see something!" I took that to heart.

The next time I actually got to implement that in my work was in my "breakout role" in *The Last Picture Show*. That's when I got my first Oscar nomination. It probably wasn't for just that specific thing,

but it did deepen my realization of Lois, who was a complex charac-
ter. It helped me to embody, dare I say it, her soul.

꧂

The books of Tony Hoagland's poems that I ordered arrived,
and I'm in love! It's so thrilling for a poetry lover to find a
new favorite poet. Here are just a few of his:

Entangle
Tony Hoagland

Sometimes I prefer not to untangle it.
I prefer it to remain disorganized,

because it is richer that way
like a certain shrubbery I pass each day on Reba Street

in an unimpressive yard, in front of a house that seems
    unoccupied:
a chest-high, spreading shrub with large white waxy
    blossoms—

whose stalks are climbed and woven through simultaneously
by a different kind of vine with small magenta flowers

that appear and disappear inside the maze of leaves
like tiny purple stitches.

The white and purple combination of these species,
one seeming to possibly be strangling the other,

one possibly lifting the other up—it would take both
a botanist and a psychologist to figure it all out,

—but I prefer not to disentangle it,
because it is more accurate.

My ferocious love, and how it repeatedly is trapped
inside my fear of being sentimental;

my need to control even the kindness of the world,
rejecting gifts for which I am not prepared;

my apparently inextinguishable notion
that I am moving toward a destination

—I could probably untangle it
yet I prefer to walk down Reba Street instead

in the sunlight and the wind, with no mastery
of my feelings or my thoughts,

purple and ivory and green, not understanding what I am
and yet in certain moments remembering, and bursting into
    tears,

somewhat confused as the vines run through me
and flower unexpectedly.

Dear Reader, do you see how it works? When a poet is stirred by something. A word, an idea, or a vision, and it leads them down a path that is pulsating with meaning, with questions, with both balms and stimulation in words. Words relating to one another in harmony, sending off shoots of other words, concepts, and feelings, and an idea is forming. You know the end of the poem is coming when what it has all been leading to reveals itself in music. The music of language, and the image appears and suddenly standing before you is a poem—perhaps a poem that contains something you needed to hear, something that may guide you in some way, something that allows you to see life in a richer or possibly even a deeper way.

ℐ

Here's another of Hoagland's poems, different in tone:

The Change
Tony Hoagland

> The season turned like the page of a glossy fashion
>   magazine.
> In the park the daffodils came up
> and in the parking lot, the new car models were on parade.
>
> Sometimes I think that nothing really changes—
>
> The young girls show the latest crop of tummies,
>   and the new president proves that he's a dummy.
>
> But remember the tennis match we watched that year?
> Right before our eyes
>
> some tough little European blonde
> pitted against that big black girl from Alabama,
> cornrowed hair and Zulu bangles on her arms,
> some outrageous name like Vondella Aphrodite—
>
> We were just walking past the lounge
>   and got sucked in by the screen above the bar,

and pretty soon
we started to care about who won,

putting ourselves into each whacked return
as the volleys went back and forth and back
like some contest between
the old world and the new,

and you loved her complicated hair
and her to-hell-with-everybody stare,
and I,
    I couldn't help wanting
the white girl to come out on top,
because she was one of my kind, my tribe,
with her pale eyes and thin lips

and because the black girl was so big
and so black,
            so unintimidated,

hitting the ball like she was driving the Emancipation
    Proclamation
down Abraham Lincoln's throat,
like she wasn't asking anyone's permission.

There are moments when history
passes you so close

you can smell its breath,
you can reach your hand out
                    and touch it on its flank,

and I don't watch all that much *Masterpiece Theatre*,
but I could feel the end of an era there

in front of those bleachers full of people
in their Sunday tennis-watching clothes

as that black girl wore down her opponent
then kicked her ass good
then thumped her once more for good measure

and stood up on the red clay court
holding her racket over her head like a guitar.

And the little pink judge
                    had to climb up on a box
to put the ribbon on her neck,
still managing to smile into the camera flash,
even though everything was changing

and in fact, everything had already changed—

Poof, remember? It was the twentieth century almost gone,
we were there,

and when we went to put it back where it belonged,
it was past us
and we were changed.

It turns out that this is a controversial poem. It has been challenged by the very accomplished Black poet Claudia Rankine, who called it racist. But I chose this poem for a few reasons. I like the way Hoagland's narrator in the poem confesses wanting "the white girl to come out on top, / because she was one of my kind, my tribe." That's not exactly racism, but it sure is bias. I remember reading somewhere that in government there are two sides: the side that believes in the individual first, and the side that believes in tribe first, and that government happens between those two sides. It's the first time that I became aware that we still have tribes, which I thought was only something that existed among primitive people. But, of course, we do have tribes: The Democrats and the Republicans are huge political tribes, but there are so many other kinds of grouping that we can refer to as tribes. I could even imagine thinking of showfolk as my tribe. I feel that we like to identify with our tribes; it gives us a sense of belonging but, of course, it is primitive thinking—and clearly in this poem, the poet was writing from the perspective of a narrator catching himself being primitive in identifying with his tribe, and the poet seems to be making fun of that primitivism.

You know I am not really one to talk about the pain of racism. I have lived the life of the privileged. There is no way for me to relate as deeply as a person who has lived their life knowing that their predecessors were enslaved. That perhaps their great-great-grandmother was forced to be impregnated by a man chosen by the slave owner, or even the slave owner himself, and she must carry the child to full term, go through the painful birth process, nurse and rear the child, and then to teach him or her how to be a good slave. I think that going through life knowing that is in your blood must be an inexpressible wound that Black people carry. But here I am talking about something that I have only read about, not something whose history I carry in my blood. Perhaps that is the difference of how white people and Black people might react to this poem. If I offend by including it, I apologize.

I never played tennis. I couldn't ever hit a ball with a racket or a bat or a stick of any kind. I could play kickball. Contact with my body and no extension, I could do. But not with any other kind of "thing." All to explain why I not only didn't play tennis, I didn't even watch it on TV. But my younger brother Steve did; he was a tennis player. And when I went to his house in California for a few days' visit, the tennis match would be on TV. This was during the competition between Martina Navratilova and Chris Evert. So, I got into the game. It seems to me now that it was pretty much a white people's sport then. And I can remember the electrifying change that happened.

Tony Hoagland wrote this poem about this transformation without being completely literal or using their real names. But anyone who was watching tennis matches at that time could recognize the change in our national attitude that happened when those two Black goddesses, the Williams sisters, smashed into our white consciousness and made us all sit up out of our complacency and recognize we were in the process of being dominated by a superior force, and it was Black, and it was beautiful.

Where I grew up in Detroit, it was all racist. You know, the N-word was used all the time.

After boarding school, I went to an all-white school back in Detroit. One day, the first Black student came into our room. When she walked in the door, I felt my heart grip because she was the only Black person. I could feel how awful that felt, to be the only anything, you know, for a child in a group. And so I invited her to come home with me after school to play, which she did. I said to my mother that we were going outside to play hopscotch, which involved chalk on the sidewalk. My mother said, "Well, why don't you play in the backyard?" I said, "No, we can't play hopscotch in the backyard. It's all grass back there." She looked at me meaningfully and said, "Play in the backyard." I said, "Why?" And she said in a low, quiet voice, "Well, what will the neighbors think?"

When I asked my new friend her name, she told me her name was Only Perkins. And when I asked her, "How come your mama named you Only?" she said, "Because I was the onliest chile' she ever had." I just love the word *onliest*, could rhyme with *loneliest*.

When Only left, my mother said, "Edna, why did you bring that particular little girl home?" And I said, "Because she's so pretty." "But she's colored," my mother said. And I said, "I know. That's what makes her so pretty."

I don't remember very much else from that time, but I certainly remember that. It always was clear to me that judging people by their skin color was just plain wrong.

At school in 1945, which was only seven years after I met Only, they showed a movie called *The House I Live In* when it was released. It's an anti-racism short film that Frank Sinatra starred in, where a bunch of boys are chasing another boy and trying to beat him up because he is Jewish and they don't want him in their neighborhood. That really affected me. I remember it so vividly. The movie made it so clear just how unfair and cruel racism is.

My friend Andre quoted something to me that he remembered anti-racism educator Jane Elliott said: "There's only one race, the human race." That the word *racism* should be struck from language.

I looked up Tony Hoagland's bio and learned that he died young, at only sixty-five, after a long struggle with cancer. This next poem I am including, it seems to me, might have been written late into the struggle.

Into the Mystery
Tony Hoagland

Of course there is a time of afternoon, out there in the yard,
an hour that has never been described.

There is the way the air feels
among the flagstones and the tropical plants
                with their dark, leathery-green leaves.

There is a gap you never noticed,
dug out between the gravel and the rock, where something lives.

There is a bird that can only be heard by someone
who has come to be alone.

Now you are getting used to things that will not be happening
again.

Never to be pushed down onto the bed again, laughing,
and have your clothes unbuttoned.

Never to stand up in the rear of the pickup truck
and scream while blasting out of town.

This life that rushes over everything,
like water or like wind, and wears it down until it shines.

Now you sit on the brick wall in the cloudy afternoon, and swing
your legs,
happy because there never has been a word for this

as you continue moving through these days and years
where more and more the message is
not to measure anything.

That verse, "Never to be pushed down onto the bed again, laugh-ing, / and have your clothes unbuttoned. / Never to stand up in the rear of the pickup truck / and scream while blasting out of town." Oh my goodness, can there be any verse that more ex-presses "teeming with life" than that? That goes directly to my heart and rings my compassion bell. Always a good thing. One of the services poetry provides. As Tony Hoagland said about "The Change," "I think poems can be too careful. A poem is not a teddy bear."

On this very topic of not being too careful, Robert Bly, the poet and major translator of many of my favorite poems, quoted another poet, Francis Ponge: "One will surely understand what I consider to be the function of poetry. It is to nourish the spirit of man by giving him the cosmos to suckle."

So here are a few poems about poetry, by poets, who are not careful:

About the Poems
Rayne O'Brian

Deep in the forest, have you ever met a
deer
 you share a gaze and before he can bolt
away
 you'd give anything if he would stay?

Then give it.

Melt. Lose your outline
Turn in your insignia of identity
The lichen of opinion, the motley of an "I"

Where you once were
the deer will enter
lie down in the lilac shadow of your breath

Scent of cedar rises
Taste of bark and blackberry
On your tongue

I think a poem can be written in this way

ℒ

I have included poems by the startlingly original poet Rayne O'Brian, who I must confess is my closest friend. We met in the 1950s at an audition. Rayne was an actress then. The audition was for *The Jackie Gleason Show*. It was during the years that he had a live show once a week on Saturday, when he played all of his wonderful characters like Reggie Van Gleason III, Joe the Bartender, and, notably, Ralph Kramden in *The Honeymooners*. He had the June Taylor dancers on his show, and he always liked to have a bevy of beauties about. That's what this audition was for, and every model in town was there.

It was held in a big empty studio and all the models were gathered in a vast room, waiting to be called into the studio to go on camera and be questioned by Jackie from the control booth.

While I was waiting to be called, I noticed this one beauty who was also waiting. She was the most beautiful girl I'd ever seen and so sophisticated looking. She wore a tight black skirt with a slit up the side, showing her perfect leg. She had on long black gloves. I was dressed in a corduroy skirt with a crinoline petticoat underneath, making the skirt puff out, in what I hoped was an "all-American girl" look. But when I saw the model in the tight black skirt and high heels, I found myself thinking, *Well if they're looking for girls like that, I might as well go home.*

We had a long wait to be called; there were many girls in front of us. At one point I found myself standing next to this very intimidating, gorgeous beauty. She spoke. She had a deep, very sexy voice. She said, "I hope they don't ask me to take off my gloves."

Oh! She's talking to me! I was surprised. "Why?" I asked.

In her deep, lovely voice she said, "I have paint all over my hands."

"Oh," said I, "are you an artist?"

"No," she replied, "I am painting my apartment." She pulled down one long black glove. "Do you like the color?" she asked. It was violet. I never saw or heard of someone who painted their walls violet.

We were both chosen to be on the show. We spent every Saturday for a full season at rehearsals for *The Jackie Gleason Show*, mostly sitting out front waiting and talking, until the evening live show. She turned out to be very smart, well-read, funny, and perceptive. And she loved poetry! We have remained best friends for more than sixty years, and now she has become a poet herself— and a spectacular one. Her poems are not like anyone else's. They are original, witty, simple, and deeply wise.

Walking Down Fourth Street
Rayne O'Brian

The day after Christmas

A red-lettered banner sashed
a fancy shop window

ANGELS—50% OFF

When the weary night janitor
packed up the manger, all angels
lost half their value.

Oh, cock-eyed world!

If the sign said, *ANGELS—FREE!*
Would shoppers stampede
knock over mannequins?

People buy angels for decoration
and receive blessings anyway

Look at it this way—

Today, a poor man can afford
his own angel—shining
above his bed.

What about the old woman asleep
in the doorway's awkward embrace
a newspaper over her head

Let her rest, officer

Who knows what silver-clad warriors
she led
over snowy Alps to victory

My trainer, Wendy, who, as I mentioned already, said, "I don't know what they're getting at" when I first introduced poetry to her, read this poem of Rayne's that was lying on a table in my apartment. "*That* poem I get," she said. I think because it was about a woman warrior. She saw herself in it.

ʓ

Poetry is not just awakening. Sometimes the awakening is intimidating. Pablo Neruda was a Chilean poet whose political stance was seen as a threat by the dictator Augusto Pinochet. When his house was illegally searched by armed forces, Neruda said to them, "Look around—there's only one thing of danger for you here—poetry."

The Poet's Obligation
Pablo Neruda

To whoever is not listening to the sea
this Friday morning, to whoever is cooped up
in house or office, factory or woman
or street or mine or dry prison cell,
to him I come, and without speaking or looking
I arrive and open the door of his prison,
and a vibration starts up, vague and insistent,
a long rumble of thunder adds itself
to the weight of the planet and the foam,
the groaning rivers of the ocean rise,
the star vibrates quickly in its corona
and the sea beats, dies, and goes on beating.

So, drawn on by my destiny,
I ceaselessly must listen to and keep
the sea's lamenting in my consciousness,
I must feel the crash of the hard water
and gather it up in a perpetual cup
so that, wherever those in prison may be,
wherever they suffer the sentence of the autumn,
I may be present with an errant wave,
I may move in and out of windows,
and hearing me, eyes may lift themselves,
asking "How can I reach the sea?"
And I will pass to them, saying nothing,
the starry echoes of the wave,
a breaking up of foam and quicksand,
a rustling of salt withdrawing itself,
the gray cry of sea birds on the coast.

So, through me, freedom and the sea
will call in answer to the shrouded heart.

TRANSLATED BY ALASTAIR REID

And this one, by Brynn Saito, an Asian American poet whose grandparents were incarcerated at an internment camp in America during World War II, as many Japanese Americans were:

Stone on Watch at Dawn
Brynn Saito

See the writer again
at the gate of memory?

The land cracks open with wind
and shots of rain.

She should drown her pages
in the sky, take to the ground
like a dogged gardener.

Turn the soil into something new—

Survive the past.

Whispers at the barbed wire
no longer suffice. What works is singing
from the cave of the self

where memories of knives
and clouds shaped like tiger faces

live together like children
unaware of their potential.

I was a child during that war. As a matter of fact, the Japanese bombed Pearl Harbor on my ninth birthday, December 7, 1941. The next day President Roosevelt declared, "America is at war!" I can still hear his voice in my memory saying those words. The country became very united then. We were all devoted to the war effort and "our boys overseas." I remember dragging my wagon around the neighborhood, collecting various items for "the war effort."

My mother worked in the Ford factory in Detroit that was converted from making cars to making ammunitions. The fury against the Japanese spread around the country. Everybody referred to them as "Japs." Nobody said Japanese anymore. There was so much suspicion of anyone Japanese, even the ones born in America, that President Roosevelt signed an executive order to incarcerate all of the Japanese people living in America, citizens or not. They all had to leave their homes and were forced to move into internment camps. There were about a hundred and twenty thousand people of Japanese descent living in America at this time.

I did not know any of this then, and I imagine many Americans have not heard about this. It was when I read this poem, and learned of Saito's family history, that I did a little research and learned what she was referring to here.

Read the poem again now that her family history has been revealed. That line, "What works is singing / from the cave of the self." Yes, that's what a real poem is, a song from the cave of the self.

*

I used to attend a kind of spiritual gathering at the end of every year, for a few days' celebration, to say goodbye to the old year and welcome in the new one. David Whyte was always part of the program. As well as being a poet, he is also a bard with what seems like hundreds of poems stocked in his impressive memory. He is an extremely handsome fella, with a sonorous voice and Yorkshire accent, and he delivers poems like an angel. I joined him in a poetry lovers' group he led on a trip to Ireland with Father John O'Donohue, who was not only a priest but also a poet. We visited Father John's ancestorial home where his family has lived and farmed longer than America has been a country. We tromped about the Irish countryside every day, stopping when our guides David and Father John felt it was time for a bit of poetry. We sat along the ledges, rocks, or grass as one of them would recite a poem, sometimes their own, sometimes other poets'. All of them lyrical and beautiful. I have already shared one of David Whyte's poems on page 60. Here is another one of his beautiful poems:

It Happens to Those Who Live Alone
David Whyte

It happens to those
who live alone
that they feel sure
of visitors
when no one else
is there,

until the one day
and one particular
hour
working in the
quiet garden,

when they realize
at once,
that all along
they have been
an invitation
to everything
and every kind of trouble

and that life
happens by
to those who
inhabit
silence

like the bees
visiting
the tall mallow
on their legs of gold,
or the wasps
going from door to door
in the tall forest
of the daisies.

I have my freedom
today
because
nothing
really happened

and nobody came
to see me.
Only the slow

growing of the garden
in the summer heat

and the silence of that
unborn life
making itself
known at my desk,

my hands
still
dark with the
crumbling soil
as I write
and watch

the first lines
of a new poem,
like flowers
of scarlet fire,
coming to fullness
in a new light.

≀

Return
David Whyte

The day started with a flurry of gulls
and a single cry, as if I had spoken
and out of the deep cave where my tongue lies,
birds were scattering in an open sky.

I went to the rail and watched them rise
over the grey clouds as if the sky were a sea
and the sea was cold now, full of shapes
and the horse-tails of winter.

And I spoke, involuntary,
out of a delighted mouth,
the old, strange word,

Ireland;
joy when uttered, grief when heard.

Father John's poems often sound like prayers or blessings, always deep and always beautiful.

Here is one of my favorites, "For Longing":

For Longing
John O'Donohue

Blessed be the longing that brought you here
And quickens your soul with wonder.

May you have the courage to listen to the voice of
     desire
That disturbs you when you have settled for some-
     thing safe.

May you have the wisdom to enter generously into
     your own unease
To discover the new direction your longing wants
     you to take.

May the forms of your belonging—in love, creativity,
     and friendship—
Be equal to the grandeur and the call of your soul.

May the one you long for long for you.

May your dreams gradually reveal the destination of
     your desire.

May a secret Providence guide your thought and
  nurture your feeling.

May your mind inhabit your life with the sureness
  with which your body inhabits the world.

May your heart never be haunted by ghost-
  structures of old damage.

May you come to accept your longing as divine
  urgency.

May you know the urgency with which God longs
  for you.

This poem reminds me of a day when I was around twenty-four and I decided, "I am going to be an actress. I am going to do a Broadway play this fall." I didn't state it like that's what I wanted to happen but as an assured event that was *going* to happen. And it did. I told everyone I knew that "I was going to do a Broadway play this fall" and then I added, "Do you know how I could get an audition?"

One person said "Yes!"

I auditioned for the leading role. The character was a model. I got the part. I began my career on Broadway that fall.

Every line of this poem is just plain wisdom in poetic form. They are words to live by. That's what I mean when I say Father John's poems sound like a prayer. They really are.

When Father John and I were in Ireland with David Whyte we visited the Yeats Tower, in Gort, outside of Galloway. Walking into the room where the poet William Butler Yeats stayed when he came there from Dublin was like walking into a quiet chapel. There was his bed, his one chair, and there the desk where he poured out his heart and his poetic wisdom. Here is one of my favorite poems of his:

The Lake Isle of Innisfree
William Butler Yeats

I will arise and go now, and go to Innisfree,
And a small cabin build there, of clay and wattles made:
Nine bean rows will I have there, a hive for the honey-bee,
And live alone in the bee-loud glade.

And I shall have some peace there, for peace comes dropping
    slow,
Dropping from the veils of the morning to where the cricket
    sings:
There midnight's all a glimmer, and noon a purple glow,
And evening full of the linnet's wings.

I will arise and go now, for always night and day
I hear lake water lapping with low sounds by the shore;
While I stand on the roadway, or on the pavements grey,
I hear it in the deep heart's core.

Sometimes when I am late for an appointment in Manhattan and my taxi driver is stuck behind a garbage truck, I curse the developer who put up all these high-rises that ruined the beautiful New York skyline from the way it was when I first arrived in the city.

They managed to make more room for people to live up in the sky, but the streets didn't change. So there are more people and more cars and more trucks but the same amount of space, and I hate being late, but there is nothing I can do about it. I take a deep breath and recite that poem by Yeats.

There are so many poems that I love. I eliminated as many as possible. They can't all be in one book. Then I reread something I'd cut, and I want it back in.

Today I read the poem "Sheep Fair Day" by Kerry Hardie from my eliminated pile. Now I want it back.

It's about God. I love poems about God, not technically religious poems but people's individual concepts of the divine—and not necessarily the father figure on a throne in heaven:

Sheep Fair Day
Kerry Hardie

The real aim is not to see God in all things, it is that God,
through us, should see the things that we see.

—SIMONE WEIL

I took God with me to the sheep fair. I said, "Look,
There's Liv, sitting on the wall, waiting;
there are pens, these are sheep,
this is their shit we are walking in, this is their fear.
See that man over there, stepping along the low walls
between pens, eyes always watching,
mouth always talking, he is the auctioneer.
That is wind in the ash trees above, that is sun
splashing us with running light and dark.
Those men by the rails with their faces sealed,
are buying or selling. Beyond in the ring
where the beasts pour in, huddle and rush,
the hoggets are auctioned in lots.
And that woman—ruddy-faced and home-cut hair,
and a new child on her breast—that is how it is
to be woman, milk-running, sitting on wooden boards
with animals and muck and death
as the bidding rises and falls."

119

Then I went back outside and found Fintan.
I showed God his hand as he sat on the rails,
how he let it trail down and his fingers played
in the curly back of a ewe. Fintan's a sheep-man,
he's deep into sheep, though it's cattle that earn
him a living.
  "Feel that," I said,
"feel with my heart the force in that hand
That's twining her wool as he talks."
Then I went with Fintan and Liv to Refreshments,
I let God sip tea, boiling hot, from a cup,
and I lent God my fingers to feel how they burned
when I tripped on a stone and it slopped.
"This is hurt," I said, "there'll be more."
And the morning wore on and the sun climbed
and God felt how it is when I stand too long,
how the sickness rises, how the muscles burn.

Then later on, at the back end of the afternoon,
I went down to swim in the slide of green river,
working up under the bridge against the current.
Then I showed how it is to turn onto your back
with, above you and a long way up, two gossiping pigeons
and a clump of valerian, holding itself to the sky.
I remarked on the stone arch as I drifted through it,

how it's dappled with sun from the water,
how the bridge hunkers down, crouching low in its tracks
and roars when a lorry drives over.

And later again, in the kitchen,
tired out, at day's ending, and empty,
I showed how it feels
to undo yourself,
to dissolve, and grow age-old, nameless:

woman sweeping a floor, darkness growing.

Just imagine how we would view the world if we were showing the
Creator how we see the divine creation. I like to say Creator rather
than have the gendered way to refer to the almighty. I learned that
Jesus spoke Aramaic and, in that language, words often have mul-
tiple meanings. The word for God is *Alaha*. It has no gender. It can
be translated in many ways; one of my favorites is "Blessed Unity"
or "Sacred Everything." It includes all, nothing is left out. That's
what I feel I want, in my consciousness: the Sacred Unity.

Whatever Man Makes

D. H. Lawrence

Whatever man makes and makes it live
lives because of the life put into it.
A yard of India muslin is alive with Hindu life.
And a Navajo woman, weaving her rug in the pattern of her
    dream
must run the pattern out in a little break at the end
so that her soul can come out, back to her.

But in the odd pattern, like snake-marks on the sand
it leaves its trail.

⚘

This next poem I've read often at spiritual gatherings because
it has such a profound message about how to view the various
seasons of life:

Shadows

D. H. Lawrence

And if tonight my soul may find her peace
in sleep, and sink in good oblivion,
and in the morning wake like a new-opened flower
then I have been dipped again in God, and new-created.

And if, as weeks go round, in the dark of the moon
my spirit darkens and goes out, and soft, strange gloom
pervades my movements and my thoughts and words
then shall I know that I am walking still
with God, we are close together now the moon's in shadow.

And if, as autumn deepens and darkens
I feel the pain of falling leaves, and stems that break in
    storms
and trouble and dissolution and distress
and then the softness of deep shadows folding, folding
around my soul and spirit, around my lips
so sweet, like a swoon, or more like the drowse of a low, sad
    song
singing darker than the nightingale, on, on to the solstice
and the silence of short days, the silence of the year, the
    shadow,

then I shall know that my life is moving still
with the dark earth, and drenched
with the deep oblivion of earth's lapse and renewal.

And if, in the changing phases of man's life
I fall in sickness and in misery
my wrists seem broken and my heart seems dead
and strength is gone, and my life
is only the leavings of a life:

and still, among it all, snatches of lovely oblivion, and
    snatches of renewal
odd, wintry flowers upon the withered stem, yet new,
    strange flowers
such as my life has not brought forth before, new blossoms
    of me—

then I must know that still
I am in the hands [of] the unknown God,
he is breaking me down to his own oblivion
to send me forth on a new morning, a new man.

The great American philosopher Ken Wilber says he doesn't regard God as a person but as a process. I like that. He cites the process of evolution where life is always evolving to its next level of complexity. I like to think, when any of us are involved in the creative process, at any level, we are mirroring the divine process to the best of our ability.

The spiritual leader of Tibet, His Holiness the Dalai Lama, was once asked what his religion was. He answered, "My religion is very simple. My religion is kindness."

I like that, and I would concur: I think that's my religion too. All the great religious leaders have talked about kindness. Muhammad said, "Kindness is a mark of faith, and whoever is not kind has no faith." Jesus's, or Yeshua's (as his name was pronounced in his language, Aramaic), preaching was basically always about kindness. Also, the Buddhist teachings include kindness.

Here are my favorite poems about kindness. The first poem, "Tikkun Olam," is by my dear friend, the poet Rayne O'Brian. *Tikkun Olam* means "repair the world":

Tikkun Olam
Rayne O'Brian

At a concert in Jerusalem
Leonard Cohen stopped
in the middle of a song
and walked off stage

His offering was not good enough

In despair in his dressing room he heard
singing
The audience—a thousand voices
sang to him in Hebrew *Shalom Aleichem*
sang him back
He played *Marianne*, tears falling
The band cried, the audience cried

Who will sing you back?

Like the man about to jump from
the high window, tell him

about the Redwood tree waiting to speak
with him for two thousand years

Sing him back

Cut one-inch strips of paper from
your notebook. Write:
You don't know how
important you are
to all of us
Write in Spanish, write in Chinese
tuck the message in people's grocery bags

Hear
the plea
in the horn of an eighteen-wheeler
to repair the face of God

Great Lord of Song
May we sing each other back

I have been friends with the poet Rayne O'Brian for sixty-eight years now. This picture was taken when I visited her in San Francisco. We live in different parts of the country, but she still remains my closest friend and one of my favorite poets.

The first play I did, *Fair Game*, turned out to be a difficult experience for me. The lead actor was very unkind to me. He knew I was new, was young, had no experience—it was my first play—and actually had no training as an actress, and he was mean. He did things like reporting to the producer that I was upstaging him. When the stage manager passed that on to me, I said, "What's upstaging mean?" I didn't know the term. The stage manager then explained that it meant that when we were talking to each other and were fifty-fifty to the audience, if I would move a little upstage, it would turn the actor away from the audience so his back would be to them. It's a trick that old-fashioned theater people used to do.

I certainly had no intention of doing that. What I was doing, I realized, was that since the theater's front-row seats curved around, those audience members were behind me, and I was blocking the actor to those people. I was only moving a little upstage so they could see him, but he led a campaign in the company that was just mean and nasty. And one day, I think it was before a show—perhaps it was dress rehearsal—the stage manager came and knocked on my door and said, "I just want to tell you that if any group of people ever did to my daughter what this group has done to you, I would kill them all."

That was a harsh thing to say, but a great kindness to me. It bolstered me in a way that really helped me to go on. A little kindness goes a long way.

Kindness

Naomi Shihab Nye

Before you know what kindness really is
you must lose things,
feel the future dissolve in a moment
like salt in a weakened broth.
What you held in your hand,
what you counted and carefully saved,
all this must go so you know
how desolate the landscape can be
between the regions of kindness.
How you ride and ride
thinking the bus will never stop,
the passengers eating maize and chicken
will stare out the window forever.

Before you learn the tender gravity of kindness
you must travel where the Indian in a white poncho
lies dead by the side of the road.
You must see how this could be you,
how he too was someone
who journeyed through the night with plans
and the simple breath that kept him alive.

Before you know kindness as the deepest thing inside,
you must know sorrow as the other deepest thing.
You must wake up with sorrow.
You must speak to it till your voice
catches the thread of all sorrows
and you see the size of the cloth.

Then it is only kindness that makes sense anymore,
only kindness that ties your shoes
and sends you out into the day to mail letters and purchase
    bread,
only kindness that raises its head
from the crowd of the world to say
It is I you have been looking for,
and then goes with you everywhere
like a shadow or a friend.

Small Kindnesses
Danusha Laméris

I've been thinking about the way, when you walk
down a crowded aisle, people pull in their legs
to let you by. Or how strangers still say "bless you"
when someone sneezes, a leftover
from the Bubonic plague. "Don't die," we are saying.
And sometimes, when you spill lemons
from your grocery bag, someone else will help you
pick them up. Mostly, we don't want to harm each other.
We want to be handed our cup of coffee hot,
and to say thank you to the person handing it. To smile
at them and for them to smile back. For the waitress
to call us honey when she sets down the bowl of clam
    chowder,
and for the driver in the red pick-up truck to let us pass.
We have so little of each other, now. So far
from tribe and fire. Only these brief moments of exchange.
What if they are the true dwelling of the holy, these
fleeting temples we make together when we say, "Here,
have my seat," "Go ahead—you first," "I like your hat."

Oh dear, this poem says almost everything I really want to say. I remember when I turned fourteen I became old enough to get working papers. My very first job was in a drugstore behind a soda fountain; however, we served more than soda. We made sandwiches, grilled hamburgers, and even homemade soup. I was the only one behind the counter, and I remember so well how good it felt to smile at people when I asked, "May I help you?" People almost always responded to me, to my smile, with their own. I felt happy that I was friendly with them, and they responded to me kindly. It made their eating their lunch alone at a counter in a drugstore a friendly event, and I liked it too. I liked their return smile.

That line in this poem "We have so little of each other, now. So far / from tribe and fire. Only these brief moments of exchange. / What if they are the true dwelling of the holy, these / fleeting temples we make together when we say, 'Here, / have my seat,' 'Go ahead—you first,' 'I like your hat.'" We are building a fleeting temple, a true "dwelling of the holy."

That moves me. Does it you, Dear Reader? If not, I encourage you to dwell upon it a bit. I have been asked if poetry is really my religion. I say no, but certain poems are like scripture to me. This is one of them. What it taught me was that I was on the right path: when I really enjoyed giving service with a smile and that a momentary kindness to a stranger builds a "fleeting temple, the true dwelling of the holy."

Oh, I want to shout that from a low-flying plane all over New York City and have it spread like a nourishing positive plague over the whole country.

Okay, Ellen, slow down. Take a deep breath. You're falling into fantasy land here. Stop!

This last poem about kindness is really a prayer.

The Hardest Part Is People
Karen Holden

So Lord, help me face them
without rancor or disappointment.
Help me see the pain behind their actions
rather than the malice,
the suffering rather than the rage.

And in myself, as I struggle
with the vise of my own desire
give me strength to quiet my heart,
to quicken my empathy, to act
in gratitude rather than need.

Remind me that the peace I find
in the slow track of seasons
or an uncurling fern frond,

is married to the despair I feel
in the face of nuclear war.

Remind me that each small bird shares atoms
with anthrax, with tetanus, with acid rain,
that each time I close my heart
to another, I add to the darkness;
Help me always follow kindness.

Let this be my prayer.

And "each time I close my heart / to another, I add to the darkness."
   Yes! Remember that! Repeat it.
   Chant it if necessary.

ف

One of the most life-changing words of wisdom I ever re-
ceived from my Sufi teacher, Pir Vilayat Khan, came when
he was giving a talk at a summer camp in the Swiss Alps facing
the snow on Mont Blanc. One summer in the 1970s he was talking
about the necessity of giving up judging. I listened to him for a
while, but I wasn't sure I knew how to accomplish what he was
suggesting. Finally, I raised my hand and asked the question on
my mind. "Pir?" I asked. "How can one not judge a person who
has been violent or abusive to you?"

He answered quickly: "Oh I am not saying that you shouldn't be discerning, but that is different than being judgmental." That gave me a lot to think about.

I found the difference in myself; when I judge, I condemn. I do close my heart. When I discern that the person behaves in a way that I don't want to be part of my life, that is a choice. It's about me, but I haven't added to the darkness with my judgment. One never really knows why a person is the way they are or why they do the things that we disapprove of. Perhaps if we knew the source of their actions or their attitude, not that we would approve of them, but we might understand them, allowing for at least some compassion.

Personally, I never want compassion to be absent from my reaction to anybody. I admit I sometimes fail at that, but it is something I aspire to. I consider it part of my credo. When I feel or hear myself being judgmental, I say (on the inside), *Stop. Turn around and go another way.*

That is exactly what this next poem is suggesting: how to turn around and go another way.

Throw Yourself Like Seed

Miguel de Unamuno

Shake off this sadness, and recover your spirit;
sluggish you will never see the wheel of fate
that brushes your heel as it turns going by,
the man who wants to live is the man in whom life is
    abundant.

Now you are only giving food to that final pain
which is slowly winding you in the nets of death,
but to live is to work, and the only thing which lasts
is the work; start then, turn to the work.

Throw yourself like seed as you walk, and into your own
    field,
don't turn your face for that would be to turn it to death,
and do not let the past weigh down your motion.

Leave what's alive in the furrow, what's dead in yourself,
for life does not move in the same way as a group of clouds;
from your work you will be able one day to gather yourself.

TRANSLATED BY ROBERT BLY

I love that line "From your work you will be able one day to gather yourself." There is something "gathering" about applying all that you have to offer and putting it into your work. I always say that a recipe for a happy life is to find a way to earn a living doing something that if you didn't need the money you would be happy to do for free. I feel very grateful that that's been possible in my life.

※

The Middle East has always had a special attraction for me. I think it might have begun while I was still living in Detroit and read *Rubáiyát of Omar Khayyám*. I came across a beautiful edition of it with glorious illustrations by Willy Pogany. The images, as well as the poems, stirred in me a yearning to visit the Middle East someday.

Many years later, I learned that the version of the *Rubáiyát* I read, translated by Edward FitzGerald, was not how it was originally conceived, as multiverses in one long poem. FitzGerald had translated many small quatrains (a unit of four lines) written in Persian by Omar Khayyám and put them together as one poem. That version of Khayyám's poetry became well-known, and it's generally considered a classic of poetry.

Actually, Khayyám is most famous today as a poet, but that was not his main identity. He was a brilliant mathematician who also had an encyclopedic knowledge of astronomy, philosophy, and, lastly, poetry. Here are a few of the verses that I have chosen out of the many selected by FitzGerald:

from **Rubáiyát** of **Omar** **Khayyám**
Omar Khayyám

VII.

    Come, fill the Cup, and in the fire of Spring
    Your Winter-garment of Repentance fling:
    The Bird of Time has but a little way
    To flutter—and the Bird is on the Wing.

XII.

    A Book of Verses underneath the Bough,
    A Jug of Wine, a Loaf of Bread—and Thou
    Beside me singing in the Wilderness—
    Oh, Wilderness were Paradise enow!

XIII.

    Some for the Glories of This World; and some
    Sigh for the Prophet's Paradise to come;
    Ah, take the Cash, and let the Credit go,
    Nor heed the rumble of a distant Drum!

XVI.

    The Worldly Hope men set their Hearts upon
    Turns Ashes—or it prospers; and anon,
    Like Snow upon the Desert's dusty Face,
    Lighting a little hour or two—is gone.

XXIV.

> Ah, make the most of what we yet may spend,
> Before we too into the Dust descend;
> Dust into Dust, and under Dust to lie,
> Sans Wine, sans Song, sans Singer, and—sans End!

XXXII.

> There was the Door to which I found no Key;
> There was the Veil through which I might not see:
> Some little talk awhile of ME and THEE
> There was—and then no more of THEE and ME.

LXXI.

> The Moving Finger writes; and, having writ,
> Moves on: nor all your Piety and Wit
> Shall lure it back to cancel half a Line,
> Nor all your Tears wash out a Word of it.

TRANSLATED BY EDWARD FITZGERALD

Sometime in the 1960s I began reading the spiritual teachings of Gurdjieff, who was a Sufi. Sufism is the mystical part of Islam. The teacher I found was Pir Vilayat Khan, mentioned earlier, who did not limit his group to Muslims only. So, in the group there were Christian Sufis, Jewish Sufis, Hindu Sufis, and unaffiliated-with-an-organized-religion Sufis. That suited me.

Through that affiliation, I was introduced to the work of the Sufi poets, including Rumi.

Here is one of my favorite poems by Rumi:

Chickpea to Cook
Rumi

> A chickpea leaps almost over the rim of the pot
> where it's being boiled.
>
> "Why are you doing this to me?"
>
> The cook knocks him down with the ladle.
>
> "Don't you try to jump out.
> You think I'm torturing you.
> I'm giving you flavor,
> so you can mix with spices and rice
> and be the lovely vitality of a human being.
>
> Remember when you drank rain in the garden.
> That was for this."
>
> Grace first. Sexual pleasure,
> then a boiling new life begins,
> and the Friend has something good to eat.

Eventually the chickpea
will say to the cook,

"Boil me some more.
Hit me with the skimming spoon.
I can't do this by myself.

I'm like an elephant that dreams of gardens
back in Hindustan and doesn't pay attention
to his driver. You're my cook, my driver,
my way into existence. I love your cooking."

The cook says,

"I was once like you,
fresh from the ground. Then I boiled in time,
and boiled in the body, two fierce boilings.

My animal soul grew powerful.
I controlled it with practices,
and boiled some more, and boiled
once beyond that,

and became your teacher."

TRANSLATED BY COLEMAN BARKS

This is the only picture of me with my beloved Sufi teacher
Pir Vilayat Khan. It's such a profound gift to know a human
being of that depth and consciousness in your lifetime.

Of course, "the Friend" in this Rumi poem is God. That is a custom in Islam, especially among the Sufis, to call God "the Friend," as well as referring to him as "Lord." I have always liked that; it makes the relationship more personal. I also like what this whole poem is saying about the discomfort we suffer as things don't go our way in life and how that gives our life flavor. I know some people who have grown up in an all-loving environment and later when life brings them disappointment, sadness, frustration, or even tragedy, they just don't know how to handle it. They collapse from the weight of the surprise blow. Someone who has grown up in less-than-ideal circumstances and has dealt with disappointment or even pain earlier in their lives has some experience sustaining their sense of self despite unexpected blows.

I am not one to say I am thankful for the frequent beatings I got the first eighteen years of my life—I don't believe any child should be dealt any painful physical punishment—but I do believe that having to learn to cope with disappointment early does prepare one for the blows that are sure to befall all of us as we continue down the glorious path of life, with all of its surprising twists and turns. And when that happens it is so good to have an ongoing relationship with "the Friend" that we can turn to and be strengthened.

ʂ

One of the perks of becoming famous is that you get invited to places you've never been but would actually really like to visit. For me one of those invitations came from Iran. This was during the time of the Shah and before the Shia Islamic Revolution of 1979. A part of that revolution was in response to the Shah wanting Iran to be more like a European city, open to American and European visitors. That's why he started the Tehran Film Festival, and I was invited as a guest of the government. As I've said, I had always been attracted to the Middle East, so I eagerly accepted the invitation. Also, I knew there were Sufi groups in Iran and I hoped to connect with one.

The American contingent spent a few days in Tehran and then traveled to the ancient city of Persepolis, and then to Isfahan, and finally to Shiraz where I learned that the Iranian people who were actually Persians worshipped their poets. I visited the burial grounds of their most celebrated poet, Hafiz, who lived during the fourteenth century. He is not buried in a cemetery but in a beautiful park, the Musalla Gardens, and to this day people come to his tomb and read and recite his poetry. The narrow path leading into the park and to his tomb is lined with roses, each one a different variety and flowering at just about nose height so that you follow the path with the aroma of roses leading to a beautiful open garden with a lovely reflecting pool.

I sat on a bench and listened to a few people reciting Hafiz's poetry in Farsi, which is the modern development of Persian. Persian is considered the best language for poetry. All the Sufi poets wrote in Persian—even Rumi who lived in Turkey. There have been many translators of the Sufi poets. The most scholarly translators aren't always the best poets. I know that one of my favorite transla-tors is Daniel Ladinsky. He's not the favorite of some scholars, but I asked the Iranian American poet Kaveh Akbar what he thought of him and he was quite enthusiastic. That was enough for me. So here is Daniel Ladinsky's translation of Hafiz's poem that I love called "Dropping Keys":

Dropping Keys
Hafiz

The small man

Builds cages for everyone

He

Knows.

While the sage,

Who has to duck his head

When the moon is low,

Keeps dropping keys all night long

For the

Beautiful

Rowdy

Prisoners.

TRANSLATED BY DANIEL LADINSKY

This poem is all metaphors, one after another. The first phrase, "the small man," now he is not talking about a man's height here, of course; he is using that as an image for the smallness of the man's mind and spiritual development. Then the next phrase, "builds cages for everyone," is an image of limitation he imposes through his judgment of everyone. The next verse "while the sage," meaning the wise man, "has to duck his head," implying heightened consciousness. "Now when the moon is low," that line gives me pause. Does Hafiz mean when there isn't enough light? Or perhaps when things aren't clear and he can help by "dropping keys" meaning helping to release people who are prisoners of their own ignorance? And the sage drops keys of wisdom or spiritual ideas that can unlock prisoners from their own underdevelopment, their limited thinking. And also the image of beautiful, rowdy prisoners has so much love in it. He doesn't call them bad for not being spiritually developed. I am reminded of what I wrote earlier about the words in Aramaic, the language of Jesus, that are usually translated as "good and bad" but really mean "ripe and not ripe." You see, he sees the prisoners, the beautiful rowdy prisoners, as just not ripe yet.

And here is another Ladinsky translation of a poem by Hafiz, "I Want Both of Us":

I Want Both of Us
Hafiz

I want both of us
To start talking about this great love

As if you, I, and the Sun were all married
And living in a tiny room,

Helping each other to cook,
Do the wash,
Weave and sew,
Care for our beautiful
Animals.

We all leave each morning
To labor on earth's field.
No one does not lift a great pack.

I want both of us to start singing like two
Traveling minstrels
About this extraordinary existence
We share,

As if

You, I, and God were all married

And living in
A tiny
Room.

TRANSLATED BY DANIEL LADINSKY

This Hafiz poem is so loving, so wise. It seems to me to be a perfect description of an ideal relationship. "How to be" in a relationship: that loving line "no one does not lift a great pack." What a way to respect whomever it is that we encounter in our lives. Because it is so true; even people who seem to be beautiful, rich, and successful, when you get to know them they each are carrying some great burden. Whether it is psychological, financial, familial, or something that we just don't know.

A girl I knew in high school is coming to mind. She was beautiful, good in school, very friendly, and she had a sweet personality. She was always smiling and very kind. She invited me to her home one day and I met her mother, who right away began to praise me and shower me with compliments. Each compliment she gave compared to her daughter unfavorably, who sat there quietly while her mother throughout dinner denigrated her. I was shocked as I watched my friend keeping an uncomfortable smile on her face, covering what must have been very humiliating for her.

Many years later I ran into her on the street in New York City. We stopped and spoke briefly. She told me she was in the advertising business. She was no longer smiling sweetly, she was tough, I'd say hardened. She'd stopped covering for the humiliation by which she was suckled, and she was hard, very hard. She had stopped covering what she had to endure in her childhood and teen years. And if you never saw behind her mask back then, you'd never know that she "carried a heavy burden."

ℒ

While I was still in Iran after my visit to Shiraz, I traveled to the ancient city of Isfahan. I was walking on a street and stopped at a red light. There was a full flock of sheep standing quietly next to me. I wondered what kept them standing so still waiting for the light to change. Then I noticed the shepherd in the front of the group. He was wearing what looked like a biblical shepherd's robe with a twentieth-century jacket over it. He had a crook in his hand that was lightly touching the front sheep's shoulder. When the light changed to green, the shepherd lifted the tip of the crook off the sheep's shoulder. And that sheep, I guess he was the lead sheep, proceeded to cross the busy street with the whole flock following him. Something I've never seen in America surely.

After dinner I checked into a beautiful old hotel. It was nighttime; I was shown to my suite, which had large French doors in the sitting room that looked out on an inner courtyard and beautiful garden. I began to unpack and suddenly became aware of a lone bird singing in the garden. I stopped unpacking and listened to the beautiful birdsong, and I wondered, *What bird sings alone at night?* Immediately the answer came: *The nightingale! I am listening to a nightingale singing alone in a garden in Isfahan.* The magical moment planted itself in my memory and my heart forever. Here's a poem about a nightingale by Rumi translated directly from the Persian by Haleh Liza Gafori:

Here, it's spring, my friends
Rumi

> Here, it's spring, my friends.
> Let's make our home in the cypress grove
> and wake our sleepy destiny
> till it surges skyward like these trees—
>
> aliens rising out of the grass.
> Just like them,
> we are bound to the ground heading to groundless ground
> where the soul flows,
> nameless and free.
>
> Here, let's take our bound souls there.

New leaf, you burst through the bark.
Tell us how to break out of our cage.

Cypress tree, you tunneled through darkness blind
and blasted through the soil.
What map was in your mind?
Tell me. I'll follow.

A flower steps out of its tight bud,
gives its nectar, gives its gold.
How do we do the same?

Soft white stars of jasmine,
sweet, dizzying musk of jasmine,
where is your garden?
I'll serve at the gate.

Dear nightingale, I bow to your bright songs,
never the same twice.
Master of improvisation perched in a tree,
flowers delight you. You delight us.
How do we pass on the favor?

Cypress tree, like a prophet dressed in green,
you whisper secrets from the alien sea.
Drawing down its pearls and coral,
adorning our ears.

Listen, you say. Listen to the flowers.
Listen to the nightingale
translating secrets into song.

Turtledoves coo at the moon.
Parrots sweeten our chatter.

The soul drinks their music,
wet and fresh as spring.

TRANSLATED BY HALEH LIZA GAFORI

Rumi says the soul drinks their music. "Yes," I say, "that's what I felt when I heard the nightingale sing in Isfahan."

Years after my visit to Iran I was invited to Turkey to receive a lifetime achievement award from the Turkish film festival in Antalya. I eagerly agreed to accept the award because Antalya is not far from Konya where Rumi lived and died and where, with the guidance of his spiritual teacher Shams Tabrizi, he developed the whirling dervishes.

After I received my lovely Golden Orange Award at the festival's closing ceremony, one of the organizers asked me if there was any other place I'd like to visit while I was in Turkey. I quickly said, "Yes, Konya."

So I was taken to the ancient city of Konya. Rumi's burial place is now a mausoleum, and the hall where the dervishes whirled and

Rumi created his poetry is now available to be visited by tourists. As the dervishes whirled or practiced what is called the Sema, he would reel off a poem and his assistant would write it down.

Rumi never wrote anything down. And he didn't preplan anything. As he was making the turn—it was not called whirling; everybody else called it whirling, but he called it the Turn—the words just came out. Interestingly, in Haleh Liza Gafori's direct translations from the Persian, none of the poems have titles. Gafori respected the original. It's not mandatory to have a title for a poem. As Rumi did the Turn and the poems came out, he didn't stop to add any titles.

He was like a prophet. A prophet of wisdom. And a prophet of human kindness because everything in him was gentle and loving.

Nobody in Konya calls Rumi by that name; they all refer to him as Mevlana, which means "Our Master." The head of the order must always be a direct descendant of Mevlana. While I was there a woman approached me and introduced herself as the fifty-second cousin of Mevlana. She then taught me what she called the Sufi greeting, which involved our hands clasped, arms raised, touching each other to the elbows, held very close to the face, so we were looking directly into each other's eyes, inches apart. I stood on the floor where the dervishes did their turning, and I recited a few of Rumi's poems that must've come to him on this very floor. This one, for instance, "Eating Poetry":

Eating Poetry

Rumi

My poems resemble the bread of Egypt—one night
Passes over the bread, and you can't eat it anymore.

So gobble my poems down now, while they're still fresh,
Before the dust of the world settles on them.

Where a poem belongs is here, in the warmth of the chest;
Out in the world it dies of cold.

You've seen a fish—put him on dry land,
He quivers for a few minutes, and then is still.

And even if you eat my poems while they're still fresh,
You still have to bring forward many images yourself.

Actually, friend, what you're eating is your own imagination.
These poems are not just some bare statements and old
    proverbs.

TRANSLATED BY ROBERT BLY

That line, "What you are eating is your own imagination," in a way perfectly describes the process of really experiencing a poem because where the poetry comes alive in you is not in the words themselves, it is the images the words conjure. It is how the imagination feeds you the meaning in pictures, in memories, and even in yearnings.

I have a very smart, educated niece, named Diane, who told me recently she has a condition called *aphantasia*, which means her brain does not form images. That's not how she thinks. It has made me curious about how my brain thinks; I definitely form images. It is one of the many things I love about poetry—the images that the words conjure in my mind. I wonder how someone who has aphantasia responds to poetry. I can't imagine. . . . *Oh! That's funny.*

After a while I got curious about what happens when Diane hears poetry. I had to call her. I told her my question and asked if I could read her a poem and she pay attention to what was happening in her mind as I read. She agreed. So I read her a very visual poem. Remember, Dear Reader, the one I introduced you to earlier in the book—"I Wandered Lonely as a Cloud" by William Wordsworth?

When I finished, I asked her what was happening in her mind as I read. She said she was hearing the words and understanding what I said. She liked the poem. She just couldn't visualize it.

"But no images?" I asked. "No," was her answer. Again I repeat, I just can't imagine that.

But it does bring up a question in me: Just how many different ways are there to be a human being?

In my kitchen, I have a little wall hanging. I can't remember buying it, but it looks Turkish. Was there a gift shop in Konya at the mausoleum? It's hard to picture that. It does not say it is a poem of Rumi's. It says, SEVEN ADVICE OF MEVLANA. I must have gotten it there. It's on silk with gold decorations. It goes:

In generosity and helping others
Be Like a River

In compassion and grace
Be Like Sun

In concealing others' faults
Be Like Night

In anger and fury
Be Like Dead

In modesty and humility
Be Like Earth

In tolerance
Be Like a Sea

Either Exist as You Are
Or Be as You Look

Hazrat Mevlana

Translated by Robert Bly

Hazrat is an honorific in Arabic and Turkish titles, used to honor a person but most especially prophets. The father of my Sufi teacher was called Hazrat Inayat Khan. So Rumi was known among the dervishes with the honorific Hazrat Mevlana.

ﻉ

Some years ago, I think I was in my late sixties, I took a trip to Bhutan led by the Buddhist scholar Robert Thurman. We visited many of the ancient temples. One of the most beautiful temples involved an arduous climb to get to. It was high in the mountains. But when I finally arrived at the top, it was well worth the effort. The view from the mountaintop was spectacular in all directions. We viewed the temple and the quarters of the monks who lived there. As we were leaving, I noticed a smaller, more modest cabin tucked away from the spectacular view. I asked, "What is that building for?" I was not surprised to hear the answer, "Oh, that's for the nuns." That's still pretty consistent everywhere in the world. The males are favored; the females are lesser.

This is the mountain I climbed in Bhutan. Unfortunately,
you cannot see the quarters for the nuns in this picture.
It was hidden behind the men's quarters.

But there is one poet who just never accepted that arrangement. Her name is Mirabai, and she lived in a totally male-dominated society, in fifteenth-century India. She devoted her life to Krishna, the Hindu god known as the "Dark One." Mirabai walked away from her arranged marriage and refused to live under the harsh limitations imposed on her and all women in Indian society. And she was a startling poet.

Why Mira Can't Go Back to Her Old House
Mirabai

> The colors of the Dark One have penetrated Mira's body; all
>   the other colors washed out.
> Making love with the Dark One and eating little, those are
>   my pearls and my carnelians.
> Meditation beads and the forehead streak, those are my
>   scarves and my rings.
> That's enough feminine wiles for me. My teacher taught me
>   this.

Approve me or disapprove me: I praise the Mountain Energy
    night and day.
I take the path that ecstatic human beings have taken for
    centuries.
I don't steal money, I don't hit anyone. What will you charge
    me with?
I have felt the swaying of the elephant's shoulders; and now
    you want me to climb on a jackass? Try to be serious.

TRANSLATED BY ROBERT BLY

Hinduism has many gods and goddesses. Many of the old religions worshipped the creator in the feminine form. One of my favorite female deities is Kuan Yin, the goddess of compassion.

Here is a modern poem about a goddess by a poet whose parents were Russian Jewish immigrants, but he was a practicing Buddhist:

The Very Short Sutra on the Meeting
of the Buddha and the Goddess
Rick Fields

Thus I have made up:

Once the Buddha was walking along the
forest path in the Oak Grove at Ojai, walking without
arriving anywhere
or having any thought of arriving or not arriving

and lotuses shining with the morning dew
miraculously appeared under every step
soft as silk beneath the toes of the Buddha

When suddenly, out of the turquoise sky,
dancing in front of his half-shut inward-looking
eyes, shimmering like a rainbow
or a spider's web
transparent as the dew on a lotus flower,

—the Goddess appeared quivering
like a hummingbird in the air before him

She, for she was surely a she
as the Buddha could clearly see
with his eye of discriminating awareness wisdom,

was mostly red in color
though when the light shifted
she flashed like a rainbow.

She was naked except
for the usual flower ornaments
Goddesses wear

Her long hair
was deep blue, her two eyes fathomless pits of space
and her third eye a bloodshot
ring of fire.

The Buddha folded his hands together
and greeted the Goddess thus:

"O Goddess, why are you blocking my path.
Before I saw you I was happily going nowhere.
Now I'm not sure where to go."

"You can go around me,"
said the Goddess, twirling on her heels like a bird

darting away,
but just a little way away,
"or you can come after me.
This is my forest too,
you can't pretend I'm not here."

With that the Buddha sat
   supple as a snake
   solid as a rock
beneath a Bo tree
   that sprang full-leaved
   to shade him.

"Perhaps we should have a chat,"
he said.
   "After years of arduous practice
at the time of the morning star
I penetrated reality, and now . . ."

"Not so fast, Buddha," the Goddess said,
"I *am* reality."

The earth stood still,
the oceans paused,

the wind itself listened
—a thousand arhats, bodhisattvas, and dakinis
magically appeared to hear
what would happen in the conversation.

"I know I take my life in my hands,"
said the Buddha.
"But I am known as the Fearless One
—so here goes."

And he and the Goddess
without further words
exchanged glances.

Light rays like sunbeams
shot forth
so bright that even
Sariputra, the All-Seeing One,
had to turn away.

And then they exchanged thoughts
and the illumination
was as bright as a diamond candle.

And then they exchanged mind

And there was a great silence
    as vast as the universe
that contains everything

And then they exchanged bodies

And clothes

And the Buddha arose
as the Goddess
and the Goddess
arose as the Buddha

and so on back and forth
for a hundred thousand
hundred thousand kalpas.

If you meet the Buddha
you meet the Goddess.
If you meet the Goddess
you meet the Buddha.

Not only that. This:
The Buddha is the Goddess,
the Goddess is the Buddha.

And not only that. This:
The Buddha is emptiness
the Goddess is bliss,
the Goddess is emptiness
the Buddha is bliss.

And that is what
and what-not you are
It's true.

So here comes the mantra of the Goddess and the Buddha, the
unsurpassed non-dual mantra. Just to say this mantra, just
to hear this mantra once, just to hear one word of this mantra
once makes everything the way it truly is: OK.

So here it is:

Earth-walker/sky walker
    Hey, silent one, Hey, great talker
Not two/Not one
    Not separate/Not apart
This is the heart
    Bliss is emptiness
    Emptiness is bliss
Be your breath, Ah
Smile, Hey

And relax, Ho

And remember this: You can't miss.

This poem is so much fun to read out loud. Actually, I recited it at a few spiritual gatherings, where I kind of performed it. I play both parts and recite it in character. And the last part starting with "So here it is . . ." I do it like a chant.

Oh, I know! I will record it that way. You won't get to see the visuals, Dear Reader, but I hope you will be able to conjure the images as you listen.

§

This morning, after many attempts at writing why I love poetry, I reread for the umpteenth time one of my favorite poems by the great Mary Oliver and said aloud to my empty room, "There! That's why!" I'll try to explain.

Here's the poem:

The Summer Day
Mary Oliver

Who made the world?
Who made the swan, and the black bear?
Who made the grasshopper?
This grasshopper, I mean—
the one who has flung herself out of the grass,
the one who is eating sugar out of my hand,
who is moving her jaws back and forth instead of up
    and down—
who is gazing around with her enormous and complicated
    eyes.
Now she lifts her pale forearms and thoroughly washes her
    face.
Now she snaps her wings open, and floats away.
I don't know exactly what a prayer is.
I do know how to pay attention, how to fall down
into the grass, how to kneel down in the grass,
how to be idle and blessed, how to stroll through the fields,
which is what I have been doing all day.
Tell me, what else should I have done?
Doesn't everything die at last, and too soon?
Tell me, what is it you plan to do
with your one wild and precious life?

First, she asks the biggest question possible—the basis of every major religion: "Who made the world?" And then she goes to the particular at hand, the grasshopper, and zooms in for the closeup and calls our attention to this particular grasshopper; what it is doing; what it looks like. She focuses our eyes for us, so we see a detail of life we've never seen before and then it is gone, it floats away, but in the meantime, we have seen like a poet sees. Then the lens widens to the bigger picture and includes not only our life, but our death, and we are left with that penetrating question: What do I plan to do with my "one wild and precious life?"

Well, let's face it, as I write to you, Dear Reader, in December 2025 I celebrated my ninety-third birthday. I have had a wondrous and very fulfilling life, but no part of me wants to sit back on my laurels (as the saying goes; it's a funny image, isn't it?) and not be open to more adventures. I loved writing this book for you. I hope I am encouraging you to open yourself to the joy of poetry. Feeding ourselves with whatever brings joy inside our hearts is good spiritual food. The prayer I say before I eat is "Oh Thou the sustainer of our bodies, hearts, and souls, bless all that we receive in thankfulness." And then I add, "I receive this food in thankfulness."

For Thanksgiving last year, I had fifteen people for dinner. For Christmas I had thirteen. Some of the same as at Thanksgiving, but not all, some different. It's difficult, it's messy, but I get lots of help. My friends bring food. My granddaughter helped cook on Thanksgiving, as she did at Christmas. These are friends I've known for thirty years or more, as well as my beloved son and his family. Having them here for holidays brings me such joy. That is what I am hoping I bring to you, Dear Reader. Joy. Poetry brings me joy. I pray it will you. Joy is the most blessed kind of spiritual food. It literally feeds the spirit.

How about you? How would you answer that question that Mary Oliver posed? "What is it you plan to do / with your one wild and precious life?"

The greatest happiness or just plain deep pleasure I've felt in my life is being a mother. I remember sitting watching my son when he was a baby and learning something new, like how to get a round object with a hole in the center to go over a stand-up peg. The concentration was total absorption as he mastered that stack of brightly colored rings. I almost cried at seeing the learning process of a human being at the most elemental level.

I learned how to be a good mother by making mental notes when I was a child that all started with "I'm never going to do that to my kids."

Not that my mother wasn't a conscientious mother. She provided me with piano, ballet, tap, and acrobatic lessons. She made all of my clothes and kept me dressed very prettily. She *presented* me. But that was an extension of her. If somebody said, "Ooh, isn't she cute?" she would say, "Doesn't she look like me?" The first time I was on the stage at boarding school, and I was reciting "Little Miss

Muffet," I heard a lady in the darkness say, "Isn't she cute?" And I thought, *I hope my mom hears that. Maybe she will take me home.* Oh, I wanted my mother so much to take me home.

When she was packing my bag to send me off to boarding school, I was pulling the clothes out of the bag, begging her, "Please don't send me away. Please don't send me away. I promise I'll be a good girl. I promise I'll do as I'm told."

I was six.

My mother wasn't educated, but she was very clever in getting what she wanted in life, if she had to. Buy the new chair, keep it in the attic, pay it off on time with money she took from her grocery budget. Make sure her husband doesn't go upstairs. "Don't let him go to the attic," and when it's all paid for, bring it down and put it in the living room. He comes home. "What's that?" "That's my new chair. *Our* new chair." "How the hell am I going to pay for that?" "Don't worry. It's all paid for."

That's the way she operated. She'd probably be running a hedge fund now. That's the kind of clever manipulation—she knew how to play him—that she was good at. She was good at getting her way. She really knew how to do that.

My mother was also a believer in corporal punishment, and she had a ferocious temper. You know what it is about those beatings you receive from your mother? You can't hit back! You are not allowed. Even though it is your body that is being slammed. It seems they have the right to really hurt it, but you don't have the right to hit back. That is so disempowering. Like you don't own your own body. They do. I confess it damages the relationship permanently. Mothers, hear me: Don't beat or even slap your kids. What you pound into them stays forever, and it ain't pretty.

But the thing is that I wrote about my mother and stepfather in my memoir. And then I found myself feeling very guilty about my mother. I don't want to hurt people who've hurt me. That's just being vindictive.

I called my mother one Mother's Day years ago and I said, "Thank you for giving birth to me." There was a long pause. And then she spoke, and I could tell she was crying. She said, "What a nice thing to say." I was surprised after my mother had been dead for quite a few years that I wished I could still call her.

So, you know, I have mixed feelings about her. That must be why I connected so deeply with Jericho Brown, the young Pulitzer Prize–winning poet, who has written about his mother:

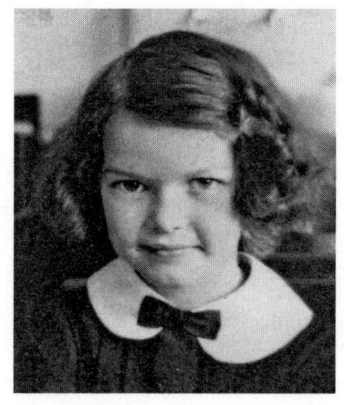

This is me at age six in my uniform at St. Mary's Academy in Windsor, Ontario. I was not a happy camper.

Hero

Jericho Brown

She never knew one of us from another, so my brothers and I
    grew up fighting
Over our mother's mind
Like sun-colored suitors in a Greek myth. We were willing
To do evil. We kept chocolate around our mouths. The last
    of her mother's lot,
She cried at funerals, cried when she whipped me. She
    whipped me
Daily. I am most interested in people who declare gratitude
For their childhood beatings. None of them took what my
    mother gave,
Waking us for school with sharp slaps to our bare thighs.
That side of the family is darker. I should be grateful.
    So I will be—
No one on Earth knows how many abortions happened
Before a woman risked her freedom by giving that risk
    a name,
By taking it to breast. I don't know why I am alive now
That I still cannot impress the woman who whipped me
Into being. I turned my mother into a grandmother. She
    thanks me

By kissing my sons. Gratitude is black—
Black as a hero returning from war to a country that banked
    on his death.
Thank God. It can't get much darker than that.

Jericho Brown converting his pain to poetry reminds me of the profound line of poetry written by the brilliant Iranian American poet Kaveh Akbar. He writes:

The first insect drawn by man was a locust.
Art is where what we survive survives.

Isn't that amazing?

Think of how locusts swarm and cover the ground, consuming everything that grows there—the farmlands' produce and the wild fields—until everything is completely gone. And then that one lone man or woman, taking some utensil, whatever will leave a mark on the cave wall, and drawing just one of the swarms that ate all the food that had been growing to feed the family for the coming year. But instead that urge to express the triumph over what could have been total destruction, made that mark.

It said, "I am here, and I have made the art that proves it."

Of course, there are other kinds of mothering in our world. Here's a beautiful poem by the US Poet Laureate Ada Limón:

The Raincoat
Ada Limón

When the doctor suggested surgery
and a brace for all my youngest years,
my parents scrambled to take me
to massage therapy, deep tissue work,
osteopathy, and soon my crooked spine
unspooled a bit, I could breathe again,
and move more in a body unclouded
by pain. My mom would tell me to sing
songs to her the whole forty-five-minute
drive to Middle Two Rock Road and forty-
five minutes back from physical therapy.
She'd say, even my voice sounded unfettered
by my spine afterward. So I sang and sang,
because I thought she liked it. I never
asked her what she gave up to drive me,
or how her day was before this chore. Today,
at her age, I was driving myself home from yet

another spine appointment, singing along
to some maudlin but solid song on the radio,
and I saw a mom take her raincoat off
and give it to her young daughter when
a storm took over the afternoon. My god,
I thought, my whole life I've been under her
raincoat thinking it was somehow a marvel
that I never got wet.

The brilliant Edna St. Vincent Millay wrote a classic and magical ballad about a supremely dedicated mother. This poem has to be Millay fantasizing about the ideal mother. Remember that earlier poem I've included called "Departure"? I suspect that poem is a confession of her real feelings about her mother, and this poem is Millay fantasizing about the ideal mother. Although I must say feelings about mothers are so complicated. I wrote in my memoir my complaints about my mother; she was not an easy woman to be mothered by. Narcissists never are—and yet she is gone now, and I miss her.

The Ballad of the Harp-Weaver
Edna St. Vincent Millay

"Son," said my mother,
  When I was knee-high,
"You've need of clothes to cover you,
  And not a rag have I.

"There's nothing in the house
  To make a boy breeches,
Nor shears to cut a cloth with
  Nor thread to take stitches.

"There's nothing in the house
  But a loaf-end of rye,
And a harp with a woman's head
  Nobody will buy,"
  And she began to cry.

That was in the early fall.
  When came the late fall,
"Son," she said, "the sight of you
  Makes your mother's blood crawl,—

"Little skinny shoulder-blades
  Sticking through your clothes!
And where you'll get a jacket from
  God above knows.

"It's lucky for me, lad,
  Your daddy's in the ground,
And can't see the way I let
  His son go around!"
  And she made a queer sound.

That was in the late fall.
  When the winter came,
I'd not a pair of breeches
  Nor a shirt to my name.

I couldn't go to school,
  Or out of doors to play.
And all the other little boys
  Passed our way.

"Son," said my mother,
  "Come, climb into my lap,
And I'll chafe your little bones
  While you take a nap."

And, oh, but we were silly
    For half an hour or more,
Me with my long legs
    Dragging on the floor,

A-rock-rock-rocking
    To a mother-goose rhyme!
Oh, but we were happy
    For half an hour's time!

But there was I, a great boy,
    And what would folks say
To hear my mother singing me
    To sleep all day,
    In such a daft way?

Men say the winter
    Was bad that year;
Fuel was scarce,
    And food was dear.

A wind with a wolf's head
    Howled about our door,
And we burned up the chairs
    And sat on the floor.

All that was left us
  Was a chair we couldn't break,
And the harp with a woman's head
  Nobody would take,
  For song or pity's sake.

The night before Christmas
  I cried with the cold,
I cried myself to sleep
  Like a two-year-old.

And in the deep night
  I felt my mother rise,
And stare down upon me
  With love in her eyes.

I saw my mother sitting
  On the one good chair,
A light falling on her
  From I couldn't tell where,

Looking nineteen,
  And not a day older,
And the harp with a woman's head
  Leaned against her shoulder.

Her thin fingers, moving
  In the thin, tall strings,
Were weav-weav-weaving
  Wonderful things.

Many bright threads,
  From where I couldn't see,
Were running through the harp-strings
  Rapidly,

And gold threads whistling
  Through my mother's hand.
I saw the web grow,
  And the pattern expand.

She wove a child's jacket,
  And when it was done
She laid it on the floor
  And wove another one.

She wove a red cloak
  So regal to see,
"She's made it for a king's son,"
  I said, "and not for me."
  But I knew it was for me.

She wove a pair of breeches
  Quicker than that!
She wove a pair of boots
  And a little cocked hat.

She wove a pair of mittens,
  She wove a little blouse,
She wove all night
  In the still, cold house.

She sang as she worked,
  And the harp-strings spoke;
Her voice never faltered,
  And the thread never broke.
  And when I awoke,—

There sat my mother
  With the harp against her shoulder
Looking nineteen
  And not a day older,

A smile about her lips,
  And a light about her head,
And her hands in the harp-strings
  Frozen dead.

And piled up beside her
    And toppling to the skies,
Were the clothes of a king's son,
    Just my size.

And the great Sharon Olds wrote this poem about a moment in mothering that we all must face at some point:

The Summer-Camp Bus Pulls Away from the Curb
Sharon Olds

Whatever he needs, he has or doesn't
have by now.
Whatever the world is going to do to him
it has started to do. With a pencil and two
Hardy Boys and a peanut butter sandwich and
grapes he is on his way, there is nothing
more we can do for him. Whatever is
stored in his heart, he can use, now.
Whatever he has laid up in his mind

he can call on. What he does not have
he can lack. The bus gets smaller and smaller, as one
folds a flag at the end of a ceremony,
onto itself, and onto itself, until
only a heavy wedge remains.
Whatever his exuberant soul
can do for him, it is doing right now.
Whatever his arrogance can do
it is doing to him. Everything
that's been done to him, he will now do.
Everything that's been placed in him
will come out, now, the contents of a trunk
unpacked and lined up on a bunk in the underpine light.

This poem is really about "letting go," which is a practice in Buddhism I learned. When I catch myself clutching something, I squeeze my hands shut tight, then while slowly opening them I say, "Letting go." I do it for anything I find myself unnecessarily attached to. Could be a thing, an idea, or a habit. This next poem is also about letting go.

⚘

ary Oliver wrote this beautiful poem about the fires that came to the woods every year near where she lived at the time:

In Blackwater Woods
Mary Oliver

> Look, the trees
> are turning
> their own bodies
> into pillars
>
> of light,
> are giving off the rich
> fragrance of cinnamon
> and fulfillment,
>
> the long tapers
> of cattails
> are bursting and floating away over
> the blue shoulders
>
> of the ponds,
> and every pond,

no matter what its
name is, is

nameless now.
Every year
everything
I have ever learned

in my lifetime
leads back to this: the fires
and the black river of loss
whose other side

is salvation,
whose meaning
none of us will ever know.
To live in this world

you must be able
to do three things:
to love what is mortal;
to hold it

against your bones knowing
your own life depends on it;
and, when the time comes to let it go,
to let it go.

I lived in Rockland County, New York, over a period of forty years, in five different houses right on the Hudson River. They were filled with beautiful antiques I accumulated for forty years. And the gardens were all wonderfully landscaped with flowers, vegetable gardens, huge old trees, a frog pond, and a couple of the houses had swimming pools. When I turned eighty, one day I suddenly said to myself: *Oh, I've been living out here in the peaceful and beautiful countryside, now it's time for a little action. I think I'm going to move back into New York City.* But could I give up seeing the sunrise over the river every morning? When you get used to living right next to the water, it is very difficult to just give it up. I was really not sure I could "let go" of that.

I spent some time looking at apartments in New York, and finally I discovered an apartment I would be happy to live in that had a beautiful view of the water. Then I had to face the fact that I was moving from a ten-room house filled with a lifetime's collection of beautiful antiques that I had come to love and feel attached to, into a five-room apartment that was considerably smaller. I'd have to give up a lot of beautiful items that had been a part of my life for many years.

One day, while musing on the problem of what I was most attached to and what I could let go of, I realized I was finding it really difficult. Everything had been carefully chosen. They were all beautiful. What do I need? What can I stand to let go? That voice inside that I call my "daimon" spoke very clearly in my head. It said, "It's all stuff, Ellen. Let go. Take what you need. Let go of the rest." So, I didn't have to choose what I liked best, I just had to furnish the new place from the current place. I stood in the middle of the living room clenching my fists tightly and then I opened my hands and said out loud, "And I let go of the rest." I did that. Left everything I didn't need in New York right where it was and had my assistant sell it all.

Of course, it's not just things that we have to let go of, it's also sometimes people. Sometimes emotional states. Sometimes bad habits. Just learning to release what doesn't serve is a good policy.

Reza's Restaurant, Chicago, 1997
Kaveh Akbar

    the waiters milled about filling sumac
          shakers clearing away
  plates of onion and radish
  my father pointed to each person whispered
Persian about the old man with the silver
        beard whispered *Arab* about the woman with
  the eye mole *Persian* the teenager pouring
water *White* the man on the phone
              I was eight
  still soft as a thumb and amazed
I asked how he could possibly tell when
           they were all brown-

skin-dark-haired like us almost everyone
in the restaurant looked like us
he smiled a proud
little smile a warm nest
of lip said *it's easy* said *we're just uglier*

he returned to his lamb but I was baffled hardly
touched my gheimeh I had bug glasses and bad
teeth I felt plenty Persian

when the woman
with light eyes and blonde-brown
hair left our check my father looked at me
I said *Arab?* he shook his head and laughed
we drove home I grew up it took years to
put together what my father
meant that day my father who listened
exclusively to the Rolling Stones
who called the Beatles
a band for girls
my father who wore only black even
around the house whose umbrella
made it rain whose arms could
cut chicken wire and made stew and
bulged with old farm scars my father my

father my father built
the world the first sound I ever heard
was his voice whispering the azan
in my right ear I didn't need anything
else my father cherished
that we were ugly and so being ugly
was blessed I smiled with all my teeth.

This poem shows me what it feels like to have a father. Something I've never known, although my mother had four husbands. The first one contributed nothing but his DNA, that was his only functioning father feat. The second was the only one I called Daddy, but he was gone pretty quickly. The third one is the one my mother married when I was away at boarding school, and he was there until I left home when I turned eighteen. As I've already written, he hated my mother's two children that he was forced to live with.

One time during a visit to my in-laws, I was sitting talking to my father-in-law and his nineteen-year-old daughter came into the room wearing shorts and a halter top. She sat on his knee like he was a chair and listened to our conversation as we continued talking. I thought, *I have no idea what that feels like*. To enter in those scanty clothes, and perch on Daddy's knee in such a relaxed manner, with no question of whether she was welcomed, or inviting any inappropriate feelings or actions from him. She was perfectly safe and unquestionably welcomed. What could that feel like? What does it mean to have a father? This poem, "Reza's Restaurant, Chicago, 1997," tells me what it is like to have a father, a real one. I have always wondered. When I'm asked what I'm most proud of in my life, I usually say that I, who never had a father, have managed to raise a son who, as my granddaughter says, "Is the best father in the whole world."

I think another reason I love this poem so much is because I remember well that for almost thirty years of my life, I walked with the feeling that I was not enough. I had to hide behind a false personality that I thought was somehow more acceptable than who I really was. It was Lee Strasberg who first "saw" me when I was taking his acting classes in a studio behind Carnegie Hall: The one hiding behind the cover story I had developed that was more interesting, more acceptable than my own self. I had gone to him to learn how to act, but he taught me how to be present and stop acting in life, so I could learn the art of acting. That process transformed my life.

In my autobiography, *Lessons in Becoming Myself* (published in 2006), I wrote about a class where we were instructed to create a sense memory—whatever we had for breakfast—so I focused on my coffee cup, to feel the outside of it.

After about twenty minutes, in my peripheral vision I saw Lee sitting in the front row, lifting up the five-by-seven white cards with an actor's name on each and going through them until he came to the name he was looking for. Then he said, "Ellen, keep on doing what you are doing, but just answer my questions."

There was a pause, and I felt the focus of the room shift to me. I tried to continue focusing on my imaginary cup, but I began to get a little nervous. What was he going to ask me?

"Do you ride horses?"

Oh man, this was from left field. Where was he going with this one?

"I used to," I answered, still trying to feel my cup, which no longer had any coffee in it. I tried to get it back.

"When you rode, did you ride well?" he asked, seemingly innocently.

"Pretty well," I said. "I used to own my own horse."

"Well," said Lee with the precision of a surgeon. "You don't have to ride that cup."

I paused. My hands remained poised, but they trembled. What had he just said? I looked at him. My exercise was over, but I found I couldn't drop my hands. The cup had become too real. I had to set it down on an imaginary table. My heart was pounding. I looked at him. He said to me gently, "What would happen if you made a mistake?"

Tears rose. What was happening to me? I was losing it. The room got deathly quiet. He said in the kindest way, "Go on, make a mistake."

I shattered, broke, chunks of my mask, my persona, fell to the floor. My bare skin, or what was under it, was exposed to the air for the first time like the pink skin under a peeled scab.

He pierced me with his gaze. He saw me. He knew me. He gave me permission to make a mistake. And I would not be punished or beaten. I could risk something. Anything. I might even risk not pleasing him. He said it was okay. I could be whatever I am. I could . . . I could . . . He said that I could even . . . be . . . myself. I cried for two weeks.

I think what this is similar to is what poets do. I think what makes a poet a good poet is that they've found a way to express themselves with their true voice. I think it is what all artists of every field do. Find a way to transform real life into art.

After two final auditions for the Actors Studio, I finally was voted in and attended the Friday acting sessions for many years. After I won an Oscar for *Alice Doesn't Live Here Anymore*, Lee asked me to moderate the Tuesday acting sessions at the Actors Studio as he continued doing the Friday sessions. I moderated the Tuesdays until Lee died in 1982, when I took over Fridays. I have been involved with the Actors Studio ever since as moderator, for a while artistic director, and for a long time copresident of the board, with the other two copresidents, Alec Baldwin and Al Pacino. I think it's almost fifty years now, and why? one might ask. It requires a lot of my time and attention that I give for free. It's my way of being of service to the profession that I love.

The great director Peter Brook said that in order for there to be theater one needs three basic things: a stage, an actor, and an audience. We provide that. Like all artists, actors must practice, especially actors who are not already established. We provide that. If an actor only acts when they get work, or even an audition, they will be out of shape. Their "instrument," as Lee called it, will not be tuned. An actor's instrument is their whole being; our past and our present. Whatever part of ourselves we deny or undervalue, those are notes not available for our work. I tell actors that when the great Vladimir Horowitz was alive, he was affirmed as the greatest living pianist. He practiced every day, eight hours a day, for his entire life. (He famously said, "If I skip practice for one day, I notice. If I skip practice for two days, my wife notices. If I skip for three days, the world notices.") Actors can't practice alone in their bedrooms. Whatever they create there easily falls apart when they get onstage in front of an audience. That's what we provide.

⚘

I recently discovered a wonderful poet named Joy Harjo. She is a member of the Mvskoke (Muscogee) Creek Nation and was named the twenty-third US Poet Laureate in 2019. Her poetry goes right to the heart without a detour. Her sensibility is refined, yet of the earth, deep, and at the same time available. She sings a song of our beloved planet Earth, the beauty of it, and the danger we all know it is in.

Eagle Poem
Joy Harjo

To pray you open your whole self
To sky, to earth, to sun, to moon
To one whole voice that is you.
And know there is more
That you can't see, can't hear;
Can't know except in moments
Steadily growing, and in languages
That aren't always sound but other
Circles of motion.
Like eagle that Sunday morning
Over Salt River. Circled in blue sky
In wind, swept our hearts clean
With sacred wings.
We see you, see ourselves and know
That we must take the utmost care
And kindness in all things.
Breathe in, knowing we are made of
All this, and breathe, knowing
We are truly blessed because we
Were born, and die soon within a
True circle of motion,

Like eagle rounding out the morning
Inside us.
We pray that it will be done
In beauty.
In beauty.

I give thanks that Joy Harjo saw that eagle's circling. I feel grati-
tude that one of the poets of the native peoples of this land wrote
a poem so we can see how she sees. How she prays. As I read this
poem, she opens me to what I can't see, can't hear but can feel in a
language that is not in sound, but in circles of motion. Wow.

And to what wisdom does the circling bring us. That we must
take the utmost care and kindness in all things. To one another but
also to our beloved planet, which we have failed to do, so that now
we have moved further beyond climate change. We are now in a
climate crisis. And as long as we go on burning fossil fuels, it will
only get much worse:

When the World as We Knew It Ended

Joy Harjo

We were dreaming on an occupied island at the farthest edge
of a trembling nation when it went down.

Two towers rose up from the east island of commerce and
    touched
the sky. Men walked on the moon. Oil was sucked dry
by two brothers. Then it went down. Swallowed
by a fire dragon, by oil and fear.
Eaten whole.

It was coming.

We had been watching since the eve of the missionaries in
    their
long and solemn clothes, to see what would happen.

We saw it
from the kitchen window over the sink
as we made coffee, cooked rice and
potatoes, enough for an army.

We saw it all, as we changed diapers and fed
the babies. We saw it,
through the branches
of the knowledgeable tree
through the snags of stars, through
the sun and storms from our knees
as we bathed and washed
the floors.

The conference of the birds warned us, as they flew over
destroyers in the harbor, parked there since the first takeover.
It was by their song and talk we knew when to rise
when to look out the window
to the commotion going on—
the magnetic field thrown off by grief.

We heard it.
The racket in every corner of the world. As
the hunger for war rose up in those who would steal to be
    president
to be king or emperor, to own the trees, stones, and
    everything
else that moved about the earth, inside the earth
and above it.

We knew it was coming, tasted the winds who gathered
    intelligence
from each leaf and flower, from every mountain, sea
and desert, from every prayer and song all over this tiny
    universe
floating in the skies of infinite
being.

And then it was over, this world we had grown to love
for its sweet grasses, for the many-colored horses
and fishes, for the shimmering possibilities
while dreaming.

But then there were the seeds to plant and the babies
who needed milk and comforting, and someone
picked up a guitar or ukelele from the rubble
and began to sing about the light flutter
the kick beneath the skin of the earth
we felt there, beneath us

a warm animal
a song being born between the legs of her,
a poem.

Dear Reader, writing this has led me to the most startling information. Fifty of the world's billionaires emit more carbon pollution in ninety minutes than the average person does in a lifetime! One study by Oxfam, an international organization, tracks the emissions from private jets, yachts, and polluting investments. Oxfam found that on average, fifty of the world's richest billionaires took 184 private jet flights in a single year, spending 425 hours in the air producing as much carbon as the average person would in 300 years. In the same period their yachts emitted as much carbon as the average person would in 860 years.

As you read in my opening letter, I do not intend to be political in this book, but recently it was announced from Washington that there is an intention to end all restrictions concerning the health of our planet for anyone investing a billion dollars in business in America. So, the very people who are creating the biggest problems for our beloved planet Earth will be given free rein to pollute it, beyond what the planet can sustain!

I remember so clearly when I first read this next poem. Every time I read it, the moment comes back to me. It was in 2011, and I was in London at the time, playing in a production of *The Children's Hour* with Keira Knightley, Elisabeth Moss, and Carol Kane at the Comedy Theatre in the West End.

I was staying in an apartment across the Thames, within walking distance of the theater. I often ate an early dinner, along the way, at one of the outdoor cafés beside the river. Often, I read poetry while waiting for my meal. I remember as I read this startling poem, there was a family at the next table with children playing beside their chairs. Boats were going by, and there was a faint breeze fluffing the leaves of the trees behind me. It was a gentle and almost bucolic setting.

When I read this poem, it was like a different and harsher reality crashed through the reality I was sitting in. And I knew the poem was true, just as the children playing next to me, the boats gently sailing by, and my happiness at being in a successful play in London were also true. I felt the complexities of the overlapping realities that combine to make our multilayered existence during our time on planet Earth.

And for all of it, I say, "Thank you."

And thank you to W. S. Merwin for writing this profound poem:

Thanks

W. S. Merwin

Listen
with the night falling we are saying thank you
we are stopping on the bridges to bow from the railings
we are running out of the glass rooms
with our mouths full of food to look at the sky
and say thank you
we are standing by the water thanking it
standing by the windows looking out
in our directions

back from a series of hospitals back from a mugging
after funerals we are saying thank you
after the news of the dead
whether or not we knew them we are saying thank you

over telephones we are saying thank you
in doorways and in the backs of cars and in elevators
remembering wars and the police at the door
and the beatings on stairs we are saying thank you
in the banks we are saying thank you
in the faces of the officials and the rich

and of all who will never change
we go on saying thank you thank you

with the animals dying around us
taking our feelings we are saying thank you
with the forests falling faster than the minutes
of our lives we are saying thank you
with the words going out like cells of a brain
with the cities growing over us
we are saying thank you faster and faster
with nobody listening we are saying thank you
thank you we are saying and waving
dark though it is

If you read this poem out loud, I imagine what happens to you is the same as what happens to me as I read it, which is you will automatically pick up speed. The poem has a built-in pace that quickens with every line. It's programmed into it, just as we (and our planet) are quickening speed as it hurtles toward climate collapse, due to the poisoning of our oceans, rivers, forests, and air, mostly due to our use of fossil fuels. However, if we continue raping our beloved planet, I don't think the bucolic atmosphere I was enjoying when I first read this poem that day in London sitting beside the gently flowing Thames will remain an available experience.

One morning, not long ago during my walk in Central Park, I passed two Asian ladies having an animated conversation. Of course, I had no understanding of what their words meant and that started me thinking about language. How certain arrangements of sounds mean one thing in one language, and those sounds arranged differently in another language make up different words and mean something entirely different, and form yet another language. That made me wonder how many languages there are and how they got started. When I got home, I consulted my handy wise man, Mr. Wikipedia, and learned that there are thought to be more than seven thousand languages on planet Earth, but nobody knows how they got started. Isn't that amazing?

Now I do know that chimpanzees who are our closest relatives in the primate kingdom communicate with one another using clicks, grunts, roars, and other sounds. Could that be considered a start of the kind of prehuman language? Then I remembered reading, many years ago, in a book called *The Monkey Kingdom*, about a four-inch-tall primate called a tarsier, who is considered "the beginning of our kind." And why? Because they have opposable thumbs. They can pick up their food with their hands and bring it to their mouths, so they don't have to lean over to smell for their food. And that position means they can sit upright, and more blood gets pumped to their brains, and they consequently have bigger brains, and that is what makes "the beginning of our kind." It makes me suspect that it was just some other kind of upper motion of the evolutionary process that resulted in our amazing development of language.

That brings up in me the question . . . is poetry actually the evolutionary development of language itself?

And that brought up the question, of all the seven thousand languages, is there one language that is best for poetry? And guess what? The answer came—Persian, the language of the Sufi poets.

And why, I ask? I love the answer. Because it is the most musical of all the languages.

Should we ever feel that our lives lack meaning or purpose, the great Austrian poet Rainer Maria Rilke reminds us to widen our lenses and have a keener view of our lives in a larger context.

This is an excerpt from the first of eight elegies:

from The First Elegy (*Duino Elegies*)
Rainer Maria Rilke

Yes—the springtimes needed you. Often a star
was waiting for you to notice it. A wave rolled toward you
out of the distant past, or as you walked
under an open window, a violin
yielded itself to your hearing. All this was mission.

TRANSLATED BY STEPHEN MITCHELL

I love that violin "yielding itself." So much richer a thought than "Yeah, I overheard a violin playing." There is no relationship there. But a violin yielding itself to me? As I happen by? What a gift!

✧

Maya Angelou was not only a poet, a memoirist, a civil rights activist, and a songwriter. She was also a singer, a dancer, and an actress.

We worked together on a film called *How to Make an American Quilt*. During our lunch breaks I used to go in her trailer, and she would recite one of her poems to me or sing one of her songs she had written. She always made me cry; her words were so moving. At the end of lunch break I would go to the makeup trailer for a touch-up, but they always had to give me all new makeup because I'd cried off the original, or I was so mascara-streaked they'd have to wipe it off and start over, which took time and made me late to the set, which is a no-no in movie land. So, I was forbidden to go to Maya's trailer. But I did go. I developed a technique to protect my makeup. I brought in two Q-tips. I'd lie on the couch in her trailer, put the two Q-tips near the corners of my eyes, then say, "Okay, hit me!" When she made me cry, I would dab away my tears with these handy Q-tips.

Maya was a great woman and a great poet. I love her magnificent poem, "Ailey, Baldwin, Floyd, Killens, and Mayfield (When Great Trees Fall)":

Ailey, Baldwin, Floyd, Killens, and Mayfield (When Great Trees Fall)
Maya Angelou

When great trees fall,
rocks on distant hills shudder,
lions hunker down
in tall grasses,
and even elephants
lumber after safety.

When great trees fall
in forests,
small things recoil into silence,
their senses
eroded beyond fear.

When great souls die,
the air around us becomes
light, rare, sterile.
We breathe, briefly.
Our eyes, briefly,
see with
a hurtful clarity.
Our memory, suddenly sharpened,
examines,

gnaws on kind words
unsaid,
promised walks
never taken.

Great souls die and
our reality, bound to
them, takes leave of us.
Our souls,
dependent upon their
nurture,
now shrink, wizened.
Our minds, formed
and informed by their
radiance,
fall away.
We are not so much maddened
as reduced to the unutterable ignorance
of
dark, cold
caves.

And when great souls die,
after a period peace blooms,
slowly and always
irregularly. Spaces fill

with a kind of
soothing electric vibration.
Our senses, restored, never
to be the same, whisper to us
They existed. They existed.
We can be. Be and be
better. For they existed.

I wish Maya and I had remained friends after the shoot, but it seldom happens that way. The way it most often occurs is you come together with your fellow actor or actors and you each have your own lives, relationships, and life circumstances that you must step out of for a period of time and build this other reality with your fellow artists. You must be in love with this person, whose hand you just shook for the first time. Or you must mother this strange little being with whom you have no relationship, that you must learn to love. Or you must be terrified of this mild man who will be dominating you twelve hours a day, five days a week for the next six weeks. You can't just say the words in the relationship, you must learn how this feels, what it consists of. What does it trigger in you? Then when the shoot is over; it's over. What this person meant to you for maybe two months every day, all day just plain ends. Sometimes you don't even say goodbye because you didn't get called on their last day, or whatever. It's just over.

Alan Alda and I were the only two actors in *Same Time, Next Year*. We became really close friends working together every day on that shoot. During rehearsals Alan mentioned how compatible we were and how it happens that we can get so close to our fellow actors during the shoot, but when it is over then it is over. He said, "Let's not do that." I said, "Yes, but we know it will happen. It always does. You have your family; I have mine. We will reenter our real lives and most likely never see each other again. Let's immerse ourselves in this relationship knowing that, and appreciating it, and being conscious that it will end when the shoot is over." After a pause he said, "You're right." We had such a good time making the film and when it was over we said goodbye. Same with Maya Angelou.

We create temporary lives, we believe in them, and then they're over. And sometimes we miss them. I miss Maya, and Alan, and Kris Kristofferson, and Charles Grodin with whom I did *Same Time, Next Year* on Broadway. Linda Blair and I stay in contact but live in different parts of the country. Marcia Gay Harden and I still talk, but again we are hardly ever in the same part of the country at the same time. She does send me a beautiful Christmas wreath every year. Mariska Hargitay and I live near each other, but our shooting schedules usually make it impossible for us to get together, although we love each other dearly. Only Rayne O'Brian, whom I met early in my career, and I stay in touch regularly.

◌

When I am excited about a poem and want to share it with a friend, I don't hand them the printed page and say, "Here, read this." I read it to them. I don't know how they're going to read it, and I have feelings about how it might be read. That's why I have recorded all these poems. I hope, Dear Reader, that you will listen to the recording and read the poems at the same time. Poetry is the music of language. You wouldn't want to familiarize yourself with a song just by reading it on the paper, would you? Of course, if you are good at it, if you can read it so the music and images of the poem come naturally to you, by all means do it! Enjoy!

After all I just wrote, here I am giving you the lyrics to a song to read as a poem. But let me tell you why.

Kris Kristofferson died around a year ago. I have a very dear memory of him from when we worked together in *Alice Doesn't Live Here Anymore*. He was a very modest man.

One time after a close-up on him, I was off camera, and he was playing to me, when Martin Scorsese called, "Cut!" Kris said to me, "Oh, what a stupid look I had on my face." I said, "Why were you looking at your face? Why weren't you looking at mine?" An expression of understanding cleared the frown from his face. He called out, "Marty, can we do another one?"

Then we really connected.

A few days later, on a Friday, he told me he was giving a concert in town. We were shooting in Tucson, Arizona. Monday, I asked him how the concert went, and he said, "Oh man, it was dog shit." I asked, "How come?" He answered, "I can't sing." I answered, "Wait a minute, I've heard you say you can't play the guitar, you can't act, and now you can't sing. What is it you do?" He answered, "I am a poet." And he certainly was. Read any of his lyrics and you'll see what I mean.

Here is one of his poems:

The Pilgrim: Chapter 33
Kris Kristofferson

(Verse 1)

> See him wasted on the sidewalk in his jacket and his jeans
> Wearin' yesterday's misfortunes like a smile
> Once he had a future full of money, love and dreams
> Which he spent like they was goin' outta style
> And he keeps right on a-changin' for the better or the worse
> Searchin' for a shrine, he's never found
> Never knowin' if believin' is a blessin' or a curse
> Or if the goin' up was worth the comin' down

(Chorus)

> He's a poet and he's a picker, he's a prophet and he's a pusher
> He's a pilgrim and a preacher and a problem when he's
>   stoned
> He's a walkin' contradiction, partly truth and partly fiction
> Takin' every wrong direction on his lonely way back home

(Verse 2)

> He has tasted good and evil in your bedrooms and your bars
> And he's traded in tomorrow for today
> Runnin' from his devils, Lord, and reachin' for the stars
> And losin' all he's loved along the way
> But if this world keeps right on turnin' for the better or
> the worse
> And all he ever gets is older and around
> From rockin' of the cradle to the rollin' of the hearse
> The goin' up was worth the comin' down

(Chorus)

> He's a poet and he's a picker, he's a prophet and he's a pusher
> He's a pilgrim and a preacher and a problem when he's
> stoned
> He's a walkin' contradiction, partly truth and partly fiction
> Takin' every wrong direction on his lonely way back home

(Outro)

> There's a lot o' wrong directions on that lonely way back home

I saw Kris at his last concert. I went backstage and asked if I could see him, and his wife said, "I'll tell him who you are. But he won't remember you." So we had our picture taken together. He just smiled. He remembered all his music. I remember reading a long time ago about people who have dementia, and they don't remember anything except the songs from when they were young.

Students used to have to memorize long poems and they can still recite them fifty, sixty years later because they had to do it. And when you're young, it sticks. Later, it slips around and leaks out.

There comes a time for all of us when things start slipping away—names, faces, places. The oldest things we memorize are etched in our brains deeply enough. It's the new things: the names of the people we recently met, along with their faces, and you find yourself saying, "Who's that? Do I know this person? Is he the one I met in the gym?" Then you smile weakly seeing if he returns a smile or nod that indicates "Yes, we have met before" or a look that says "Hello, stranger" or just a turn away that indicates he has no idea why you are nodding or smiling at him.

The names are another matter. The longer I have known them, the surer their names. It's the recent ones that are mostly unavailable to me.

With my dear friend
Kris Kristofferson.

꙳

Billy Collins wrote a phenomenal poem about memory called "Forgetfulness."

Forgetfulness
Billy Collins

The name of the author is the first to go
followed obediently by the title, the plot,
the heartbreaking conclusion, the entire novel
which suddenly becomes one you have never read, never
    even heard of,

as if, one by one, the memories you used to harbor
decided to retire to the southern hemisphere of the brain,
to a little fishing village where there are no phones.

Long ago you kissed the names of the nine muses goodbye
and watched the quadratic equation pack its bag,
and even now as you memorize the order of the planets,

something else is slipping away, a state flower perhaps,
the address of an uncle, the capital of Paraguay.

Whatever it is you are struggling to remember,
it is not poised on the tip of your tongue
or even lurking in some obscure corner of your spleen.

It has floated away down a dark mythological river
whose name begins with an L as far as you can recall

well on your way to oblivion where you will join those
who have even forgotten how to swim and how to ride
    a bicycle.

No wonder you rise in the middle of the night
to look up the date of a famous battle in a book on war.
No wonder the moon in the window seems to have drifted
out of a love poem you used to know by heart.

"A love poem you used to know by heart." Isn't that a beautiful combination of words? It made me wonder where the phrase "to know by heart" came from. I looked it up, with a bit of help from AI, and learned that it is a very old phrase to describe the process of memorizing because long ago it was thought that the heart was the center of memory and the intellect. The phrase can be traced back as early as 1525; it makes me wonder when we humans realized all the brain can do. I guess we are still learning that.

    I was blessed with a good memory. Memorizing always came easy to me. If I read something a few times, I pretty much knew it. Well, let me say, that's the way it always was. Now in my tenth decade, not so much. I must drill now, go over and over whatever it is that I am trying to lodge in there. I remember visiting the great British actor John Gielgud in his dressing room after I saw him in a play in London. We had a conversation about memory. He said, "The memory is a muscle, and like any muscle it needs to be exercised." He said, "I memorize something every day: My role if I'm in a play or a poem if I am not. Or at the very least"—imagine the last phrase in a strong British accent—"a column of newspaper print" (newspaper spelled *neoospapeh*).

I worked with another British actor who shall remain nameless, and he had his lines on cards all over the set. When he was speaking to me on a close-up, I would be holding the card with his line on it, in front of my face. But he was a heavy drinker.

Alcohol is the enemy of the actor.

I used to drink alcohol, but I gave it up sometime in my early forties, when I gave up all my bad habits. Alcohol, grass, and meat among others.

At some point in my teens, when I realized that a hamburger was a ground-up dead cow, I lost my taste for meat. There were short periods in my life when I could stand to eat meat, but mostly it was pretty repulsive to me.

For a while, I was eating chicken, but one day I was visiting the home of my friend, Marnie Andrews, in upstate New York. I was taking a walk from her house in the mountains, and I passed a neighbor's house that had chickens walking around on her property.

They were very beautiful, different colors with long tails curling up over their backs. As they walked toward me for a friendly look, I thought, *Oh, they are so beautiful.* Then the next thought was, *Oh, great, now I can't eat chickens anymore!*

I haven't eaten chicken since.

A few years ago, I was giving a talk in some big ballroom in New York, and afterward a woman walked up to me and said, "Okay, I know how old you are." I was somewhere in my eighties at the time. She said, "What's your secret?" I answered, "I don't drink, I don't smoke, I eat a healthy diet, and I exercise daily."

She screwed up her face, and in a deflated tone, she said, "Oh, *you don't drink?*"

Some people want the results of good life choices, but they expect the results are available without changing their habits. It doesn't work that way. I was tempted to recite to her the Rilke poem "Archaic Torso of Apollo."

Archaic Torso of Apollo
Rainer Maria Rilke

We cannot know his legendary head
with eyes like ripening fruit. And yet his torso
is still suffused with brilliance from inside,
like a lamp, in which his gaze, now turned to low,

gleams in all its power. Otherwise
the curved breast could not dazzle you so, nor could
a smile run through the placid hips and thighs
to that dark center where procreation flared.

Otherwise this stone would seem defaced
beneath the translucent cascade of the shoulders
and would not glisten like a wild beast's fur:

would not, from all the borders of itself,
burst like a star: for here there is no place
that does not see you. You must change your life.

TRANSLATED BY STEPHEN MITCHELL

It's like the focus is on the torso and then all of a sudden the focus turns around and announces "You must change your life." That's what that woman didn't want to do. She didn't want to make the effort to really change her life.

Speaking of Marnie Andrews and her lovely house in the mountains, she happens to be a beautiful actress, a wonderful, respected director, and a poet. Here's a poem she wrote about that same walk I took when I saw the chickens:

Little Things on This Big Day
Marnie Andrews

It begins as yesterday ended,
another day of gray,
then lifts, each turn
contributes to the shift.

First,
a pair of squirrels
lay flat against the
bark of the maple
sunning themselves,
one on the other's back
massages, picking
through her friend's fur,
checking for tiny ticks, or
any other things that itch.

Then, there, that bird call
wasn't here a day ago.
And gold starts to show
in finch feathers at the feeder.

Yes, the wind blows cold,
stunning in a crisp sight.
It whips the air of yellow light
against evolving blues of sky.

No need to analyze
why the day has this power,
an ode forms
in one who walks
the empty road.

Further up, wind turns to waves
washing through pines,
tuning their needles to hold sway.
The creek, named for one gone,
sings its song in water
flowing down the crevice.

The rotting trunk's colors
magnify the shifts. New
puffs of air, alive with
the breaths of all who
expelled it to walk
up this hill,
they will themselves
higher to see more.

This day is like no other,
though eras of days
precede it.
It holds the spirit,
then rolls a body in
a coverlet to nap
in the afternoon sun.

Later,
on waking,
the power in the house
is gone from a wind so
big it felled trees
onto lines of electricity.

The day ends,
its magic spun,
Its vigor fades
its work,
done.

The beautiful line "An ode forms / in one who walks / an empty road. . . ." Only a person who is a born poet can, in my opinion, think like that. Remember the poet David Whyte you read about earlier, who wrote something in the same vein: "It happens to those who live alone." Perhaps lines from a possible poem go off in many of us. But our ear is not that attuned to our inner poem that wants to be born.

This poem of Marnie's is just as wonderfully attuned:

For
Marnie Andrews

> For the bear who ate the only apple on the tree.
> For the dog buried near there. For furry
> companions buried everywhere.
> For the friends who stayed
> and ones who went away.
>
> For parents, grandparents,
> the ancestors who still guide,
> for the child I still want to know
> who parents now. For those
> young ones he sees grow.
>
> For the ghost who left and
> returns again at both
> right and
> inappropriate times.

For all the ghosts,
alive and dead,
who swim in my
head when I
want contact.
For those times when
they crowd into
the empty room.

For the times I long to be alone
and when I fear it. For the girl inside
who thinks she can't survive and
the woman who knows
she won't in time.

For the way words come
to wash away the pain
to clearly see
what joy remains.

The facts of aging slowly come upon us. We usually notice it in our body first, or maybe our face for an actor or for someone else whose appearance is part of their profession. As we age, we don't just lose our eyesight and our hearing—we also sometimes lose our facial recognition.

The Coming of Wisdom with Time
William Butler Yeats

> Though leaves are many, the root is one;
> Through all the lying days of my youth
> I swayed my leaves and flowers in the sun;
> Now I may wither into the truth.

But however it comes, the awareness of our aging demands a certain maturity to handle without whining too much.

This next poem by Fleur Adcock, who was born in New Zealand, seems to me to express a mature and wise attitude toward aging:

Weathering
Fleur Adcock

Literally thin-skinned, I suppose, my face
catches the wind off the snow-line and flushes
with a flush that will never wholly settle. Well:
that was a metropolitan vanity,
wanting to look young for ever, to pass.

I was never a pre-Raphaelite beauty,
nor anything but pretty enough to satisfy
men who need to be seen with passable women.
But now that I am in love with a place
which doesn't care how I look, or if I'm happy,

happy is how I look, and that's all.
My hair will turn grey in any case,
my nails chip and flake, my waist thicken,
and the years work all their usual changes.
If my face is to be weather-beaten as well

that's little enough lost, a fair bargain
for a year among lakes and fells, when simply
to look out of my window at the high pass
makes me indifferent to mirrors and to what
my soul may wear over its new complexion.

Oh that line "what / my soul may wear over its new complexion." Isn't that a potent line? It takes the attention away from the surface, the complexion, and pulls you right into essence. See, that's what I mean about poetry. It can do that. Take you right under the surface, to the soul in a few words.

That word *fells* she uses, I didn't know that word, so I looked it up. In case you don't know what it means, it's an old English word that means "high undeveloped land."

And here's a wonderful Chinese poem written in the twelfth century by Wu-Men. China has a long history of poetry:

Ten thousand flowers in spring, the moon in autumn
Wu-Men

> Ten thousand flowers in spring, the moon in autumn,
> a cool breeze in summer, snow in winter
> If your mind isn't clouded by unnecessary things,
> this is the best season of your life.

TRANSLATED BY STEPHEN MITCHELL

The great thing about this poem is that it can relate to every season of your life.

~

I must include another poem by the amazing Billy Collins who has been dubbed "the most popular American poet." This poem of his, "The Parade," points to a period in life when we begin to grow aware that life doesn't go on forever:

The Parade
Billy Collins

How exhilarating it was to march
along the great boulevards
in the sunflash of trumpets
and under all the waving flags—
the flag of desire, the flag of ambition.

So many of us streaming along—
all of humanity, really—
moving in perfect sync,
yet each lost in the room of a private dream.

How stimulating the scenery of the world,
the rows of roadside trees,
the huge blue sheet of the sky.

How endless it seemed until we veered
off the broad turnpike
into a pasture of high grass,
headed toward the dizzying cliffs of mortality.

Generation after generation,
we shoulder forward
under the play of clouds
until we high-step off the sharp lip into space.

So I should not have to remind you
that little time is given here
to rest on a wayside bench,
to stop and bend to the wildflowers,
or to study a bird on a branch—

not when the young
keep shoving from behind,
not when the old are tugging us forward,
pulling on our arms with all their feeble strength.

The great Mary Oliver has been my soul teacher in so many ways. Her greatest gift of all is her illumination about death, "When Death Comes":

When Death Comes
Mary Oliver

When death comes
like the hungry bear in autumn;
when death comes and takes all the bright coins from his purse

to buy me, and snaps the purse shut;
when death comes
like the measle-pox;

when death comes
like an iceberg between the shoulder blades,

I want to step through the door full of curiosity, wondering:
what is it going to be like, that cottage of darkness?

And therefore I look upon everything
as a brotherhood and a sisterhood,
and I look upon time as no more than an idea,
and I consider eternity as another possibility,

and I think of each life as a flower, as common
as a field daisy, and as singular,

and each name a comfortable music in the mouth,
tending, as all music does, toward silence,

231

and each body a lion of courage, and something
precious to the earth.

When it's over, I want to say: all my life
I was a bride married to amazement.
I was the bridegroom, taking the world into my arms.

When it's over, I don't want to wonder
if I have made of my life something particular, and real.
I don't want to find myself sighing and frightened,
or full of argument.

I don't want to end up simply having visited this world.

Yes, that's it! That line "I want to step through the door full of cu-
riosity." Yes. Yes! That's the way I pray to go. I know people don't
like to talk about death or read about it, for that matter. But I feel
I must. We can't really avoid it, however much we would like to.
So let's have our wisdom bag packed for when the time comes to
go . . . and it will come. Keeping it in our awareness also helps us
live more fully and consciously. Helps us to . . . as the poet Mach-
ado said, "Wake up!"

Recently, I was in the charming, historic city of Venice, Italy. I was
sitting in my suite in a lovely old hotel on a rainy day. The previous
day I had been presented with the Liberatum Pioneer Award for

my "contribution in advancing society through the arts." In giving my thanks, I recited (with notes in my hand) Mary Oliver's poem. I announced beforehand for them not to be put off by the title, that they would understand why I was reading this poem to them by the end, and then I said, "Its title is 'When Death Comes.'" It finished with the line "I don't want to end up simply having visited this world." Then I said, "By giving me this award you have assured me that I haven't just visited this world, and for that I am profoundly grateful."

Somehow poetry always says it a little better than just plain talk. There is something so satisfying to say something meaningful in a poetic way. It adds beauty to the statement.

Oh! And there's a thought: The great Sufi master Hazrat Inayat Khan says that one of the surest ways to love God is to love beauty. That, of course, does not mean simply human beauty, but beauty in nature, in art, in aesthetics, in music, and in all ways that the world manifests beauty.

It was a lovely ceremony. I was so pleased to see, before they gave me the award, that they had the beautiful Taylor Russell (a Mary Oliver lover) share a speech she wrote about working with me in a film called *Mother Couch*.

At the beginning of filming, I noticed a collection of Mary Oliver poems on her chair. I knew right away I was going to like this girl.

When we (I traveled with my assistant Caitlin) left Venice, we took the train to Rome. We were there for three days. It was summer, school was out, so it was tourist time. The city was remarkably

233

crowded. It was so overrun with tourists it broke my heart. The Colosseum and the Vatican were like Disneyland while we were there.

Nevertheless, the highlight of our time there was a visit to the Villa Borghese to once again view that magnificent Bernini sculpture, "Apollo and Daphne." The moment we entered the room, and I saw what we were approaching, I was immediately flooded with tears. We were joined by a small group with a guide, and she led us to it and began talking about the work, but her voice faded from my first level of attention and was superseded by the poem I heard inside of me.

"Why do you follow me? / Any moment I can be / Nothing but a laurel-tree."

And suddenly my whole life was like an accordion. There was this moment with me standing there, part of a gift from the givers of the Liberatum Pioneer Award. At the same time there was the me that stood there in 1970, when I first saw this magnificent work. And also, there was the high school girl that first memorized that Millay poem and has carried it alive in herself—myself, I mean—for maybe seventy-five years or so, all together standing there, lightly crying but in rapture.

A beloved poem that you carry inside is a gift that keeps on giving.

While we were in Rome, I visited a place I had never visited before but always wanted to. It's a small museum on the side of the Spanish Steps that once was the apartment where poets Keats and Shelley lived, and Keats died there at the age of twenty-five from tuberculosis. I had read some of their work and though I admired it, I had never memorized a poem by either of them. Inside the beautiful little apartment, one room has been converted to a bookstore that sells their books. I bought a book called *John Keats and Percy Bysshe Shelley* to familiarize myself with their work, which I really didn't know. But to my surprise I came upon this poem, and I suddenly remembered it was one of the early poems I read that moved me, probably around seventy years ago in Detroit.

Ozymandias
Percy Bysshe Shelley

> I met a traveller from an antique land
> Who said: "Two vast and trunkless legs of stone
> Stand in the desert. . . . Near them, on the sand,
> Half sunk, a shattered visage lies, whose frown,
> And wrinkled lip, and sneer of cold command,
> Tell that its sculptor well those passions read
> Which yet survive, stamped on these lifeless things,
> The hand that mocked them, and the heart that fed:
> And on the pedestal, these words appear:

My name is Ozymandias, King of Kings:
Look on my works, ye Mighty, and despair!
Nothing beside remains. Round the decay
Of that colossal Wreck, boundless and bare
The lone and level sands stretch far away.

I remember so well that this was the poem that first cautioned me to remember that no matter how famous and powerful one can become in their lifetime, and how many awards they get, it is possible after they are gone, all that they've achieved can be forgotten.

I'd forgotten that.

ℒ

This next poem was written by John O'Neill, who is a published poet, as well as a spiritual teacher. We met when we were both involved with the Sufis. Now he is the codirector of Awaken Heart School in Albany, New York.

One day years ago he was at my house and he used the phrase "body of resurrection." I had never heard the phrase before, and I called him the next day and told him I would like to learn more about it. He answered, "I'll write something for you." A few days later this poem arrived in the mail. It has become my all-time favorite poem. I have recited it many times, in various spiritual gatherings.

Very often people have asked for a copy of it. I called John and asked him if I had his permission to give people copies. He answered, "You don't need my permission, Ellen. The poem is yours. I wrote it for you. And I gave it to you."

That is the most generous thing I have ever heard a writer do. To give away his work like that.

Growing the Body of Resurrection
John O'Neill

> We grow ourselves day by day
> mostly hidden from view—
> deep in the mountain's veins—
> like the crystal's silent accretion
> one molecule at a time.
>
> We grow ourselves day by day
> like the butterfly
> whose orange and black wings
> are hidden in the silky sheath,
> hanging seemingly unchanged
> from a branch in the garden.
>
> Have faith in the wounds
> that penetrate our opaque shells—

as the farmer's plow
opens the earth for seed—
the wounds that turn
our guarded inside tender
and fertile for growth.

Have faith in the power
that pushes fragile seeds, sun-seeking,
through the dark and heavy earth.

Have faith in the light
that fills the new moon's darkness,
the sliver that grows, almost unperceived,
night after night,
into its true form.

This is the way we grow:
by choice, by chance, by design,
by fate, by faith—
in all ways our life is rendered
into an undying fragrance,
the sacred fragrance that perfumes eternity.

And so, Dear Reader, I have come to the final pages I am writing to you, in hopes that I have been able to share some of the love I feel for poetry. And I also want to share one more thing with you before we part. It's not a poem, but it is about a couple of things that have come up since I have been writing.

First of all, I was in the Metropolitan Museum of Art to celebrate my birthday in 2024 with some close friends, a tradition I established many years ago. While in the very crowded large main hall of the entrance, where I was waiting for my friends to gather, a woman walked by me wearing a very unusual patchwork coat. I had never seen one like it before. I decided to tell her. I approached her and I said, "I like your coat." She turned to me and I added, "It's beautiful." She smiled at me and she said, "I like your smile, that's what's beautiful." And for a split second we recognized each other. I could tell she wasn't looking at the actress. It was a full moment of one that I quoted earlier in the poem "Small Kindnesses": "Only these brief moments of exchange. / What if they are the true dwelling of the holy, these / fleeting temples we make together, when we say 'Here / have my seat,' or 'Go ahead—you first,' or 'I like your hat.'"

You see, this is what it meant in the "Growing the Body of Resurrection" "by choice, by chance, by design, / by fate, by faith." That's what this last poem means to me. Our day-to-day, moment-by-moment intention to be kind and to be conscious. To build in ourselves faith. "Faith in the wounds / that penetrate our opaque shells— / as the farmer's plow / opens the earth for seed— /

the wounds that turn / our guarded inside tender / and fertile for growth," so we can soften to our beloveds, but also to strangers, and especially to ourselves so that we can learn how to simply manifest our own authentic selves. And I love the idea of the last line, that what we release from our bodies as our spirits exit is a "sacred fragrance that perfumes eternity."

And finally, two poems by my longest and dearest friend, Rayne O'Brian, who writes about death—and then in the last poem—about what happens after.

If Death Had a Camera
Rayne O'Brian

> If death had a camera
> and I had five minutes—what would I do?
> *Omigod*
> What would I wear?

Earrings? Or not?
Sheathed in starry sequins
cool on a black-lacquer bar stool
making a fist, raising my perfectly
manicured middle finger and punching up
—my message for all eternity

Or

a penitent, clad in simple cotton
of sinless blue like the shadow
of a lamb. Sandals from the weary racks
of the Salvation Army

Wait!!
It's late. Tell the truth

I would do what I always do—
Try and make him love me

Why Ghosts Wear Sheets
Rayne O'Brian

Only new ghosts wear sheets
Sheets are just training togs
The novice still clings, longs for
music, kisses and cake

You can't just die and
be a ghost right away
You gotta go to school—
be certified

First you learn to lurk
purple a shadow
sway a curtain
when no breeze blows

When you're dead six months
you can work Halloween

After a year—Advanced Pranks

You go diaphanous
Haunt Houses I and II
scent the air with jasmine or rose
Learn border etiquette for cemeteries

Refine your gift

At the highest level you are named
Messenger, and then you can enter
dreams
nudge objects

This morning on my walk
a willow branch bent low before me
scattering light at my feet

That was you, wasn't it

Acknowledgments

I want to thank my agents at United Talent Agency, Albert Lee and Gráinne Fox, who, knowing I was a poetry lover, first suggested to me that I write a book about poetry and introduced me to Judith Curr, president of the HarperOne Group, along with Elizabeth Mitchell, who became my able editor.

And Karen Moline, who read an early draft and asked such stimulating questions. She inspired me to write more and write better, and then introduced me to that amazing speech by John F. Kennedy that I quoted for a preface.

I love this opportunity to publicly thank my manager Courtney Kivowitz for guiding my career for the past twenty-six years.

I still write longhand, so it has been the work of my previous assistant Sierra Byrons and my present assistant Caitlin Brown to transform my scrawl to proper technologically produced text on a computer.

And lastly, I thank my son, Jefferson Jack Burstyn, for being a living angel in my life and, with his beautiful wife, Patricia, for providing me with the blessing of my one grandchild, Emily Burstyn.

Credits & Permissions

Edna St. Vincent Millay, "Love is not all: it is not meat nor drink" and "Not in a silver casket cool with pearls" from *Collected Poems*. Copyright 1931, © 1958 by Edna St. Vincent Millay and Norma Millay Ellis. Reprinted with the permission of The Permissions Company LLC on behalf of Holly Peppe, Literary Executor, The Edna St. Vincent Millay Society, millay.org.

Mirabai, "Why Mira Can't Go Back to Her Old House," translated by Robert Bly, from *The Winged Energy of Delight: Selected Translations*. Copyright © 2004 by Robert Bly. Used by permission of Georges Borchardt Inc. on behalf of the translator's estate and HarperCollins Publishers.

Portia Nelson, "Autobiography in Five Short Chapters" from *There's a Hole in My Sidewalk: The Romance of Self-Discovery*. Copyright © 1977, 1993 by Portia Nelson. Reprinted with the permission of Beyond Words/Atria Books, an imprint of Simon & Schuster LLC. All rights reserved.

Pablo Neruda, "The Poet's Obligation" from *Fully Empowered*, translated by Alastair Reid. Copyright © 1975 by Alastair Reid. Reprinted by permission of Farrar, Straus & Giroux LLC.

Naomi Shihab Nye, "Kindness" from *Words Under the Words: Selected Poems*. Copyright © 1994 by Naomi Shihab Nye. Used with permission of Far Corner Books.

Rayne O'Brian, "Love Dogs," "Divest," and "If Death Had a Camera" (all previously uncollected). "Walking Down Fourth Street," "Tikkun Olam," and "Why Ghosts Wear Sheets" from *Living on a Song a Day* (Blue Light Press, 2021). Copyright © 2021 by Rayne O'Brian. Reprinted with the permission of the author.

John O'Donohue, "For Longing" from *To Bless the Space Between Us: A Book of Blessings*. Copyright © 2008 by John O'Connor. Used by permission of Doubleday, an imprint of the Knopf Doubleday Publishing Group, a division of Penguin Random House LLC. All rights reserved.

Sharon Olds, "The Summer-Camp Bus Pulls Away from the Curb" from

List of Poems

"Invictus," William Ernest Henley

"The Poet," David Whyte

"Departure," Edna St. Vincent Millay

"Daphne," Edna St. Vincent Millay

"Not in a silver casket cool with pearls," Edna St. Vincent Millay

"Renascence," Edna St. Vincent Millay

"Love is not all: it is not meat nor drink," Edna St. Vincent Millay

"The Journey," Mary Oliver

"The Death of Lovers," Charles Baudelaire

"New Year Poem," Mary Sarton

"Souvenir," Edna St. Vincent Millay

"Annabel Lee," Edgar Allan Poe

"The Bells," Edgar Allan Poe

LIST OF POEMS

"The Raven," Edgar Allan Poe

"I Have No Idea Where I Am Going," Thomas Merton

"Self-Portrait," David Whyte

"Autobiography in Five Short Chapters," Portia Nelson

"Benedictio," Edward Abbey

"I Wandered Lonely as a Cloud," William Wordsworth

"Vespers," Louise Glück

"Matins," Louise Glück

"Love Dogs," Rumi

"Love Dogs," Rayne O'Brian

"Disappointment," Tony Hoagland

"The Guest House," Rumi

from *Proverbs and Tiny Songs*, Antonio Machado

"A Few Words on the Soul," Wisława Szymborska

"Entangle," Tony Hoagland

"The Change," Tony Hoagland

"Into the Mystery," Tony Hoagland

"About the Poems," Rayne O'Brian

"Walking Down Fourth Street," Rayne O'Brian

"The Poet's Obligation," Pablo Neruda

"Stone on Watch at Dawn," Brynn Saito

"It Happens to Those Who Live Alone," David Whyte

"Return," David Whyte

"For Longing," John O'Donohue

"The Lake Isle of Innisfree," William Butler Yeats

"Sheep Fair Day," Kerry Hardie

"Whatever Man Makes," D. H. Lawrence

"Shadows," D. H. Lawrence

"Tikkun Olam," Rayne O'Brian

"Kindness," Naomi Shihab Nye

"Small Kindnesses," Danusha Laméris

"The Hardest Part Is People," Karen Holden

"Throw Yourself Like Seed," Miguel de Unamuno

from *The Rubáiyát of Omar Khayyám*, Omar Khayyám

"Chickpea to Cook," Rumi

"Dropping Keys," Hafiz

"I Want Both of Us," Hafiz

"Here, it's spring, my friends," Rumi

"Eating Poetry," Rumi

"Why Mira Can't Go Back to Her Old House," Mirabai

"The Very Short Sutra on the Meeting of the Buddha and the Goddess," Rick Fields

"The Summer Day," Mary Oliver

"Hero," Jericho Brown

"The Raincoat," Ada Limón

"The Ballad of the Harp-Weaver," Edna St. Vincent Millay

"The Summer-Camp Bus Pulls Away from the Curb," Sharon Olds

"In Blackwater Woods," Mary Oliver

"Reza's Restaurant, Chicago, 1997," Kaveh Akbar

"Eagle Poem," Joy Harjo

"When the World as We Knew It Ended," Joy Harjo

"Thanks," W. S. Merwin

from The First Elegy (*Duino Elegies*), Rainer Maria Rilke

"Ailey, Baldwin, Floyd, Killens, and Mayfield (When Great Trees Fall)," Maya Angelou

"The Pilgrim: Chapter 33," Kris Kristofferson

"Forgetfulness," Billy Collins

"Archaic Torso of Apollo," Rainer Maria Rilke

"Little Things on This Big Day," Marnie Andrews

"For," Marnie Andrews

"The Coming of Wisdom with Time," William Butler Yeats

"Weathering," Fleur Adcock

"Ten thousand flowers in spring, the moon in autumn," Wu-Men

"The Parade," Billy Collins

"When Death Comes," Mary Oliver

"Ozymandias," Percy Bysshe Shelley

"Growing the Body of Resurrection," John O'Neill

"If Death Had a Camera," Rayne O'Brian

"Why Ghosts Wear Sheets," Rayne O'Brian